JUST AN ORDINARY PERSON

A MEMOIR

DIANE ORTON

Copyright © 2020 by Diane Orton
All rights reserved.

TABLE OF CONTENTS

Foreword		4
1	On being a mother	8
2	My family of origin	10
3	Ah yes, I remember it well	27
4	Seven to seventeen	45
5	Tertiary studies and extracurricular activities	67
6	Marriage and motherhood	83
7	A new relationship and a new country	106
8	A move, an affair, and a 'handicapped' child	121
9	Fun and games as children play	133
10	Unexpected and unwelcome events	142
11	Things of the spirit	150
12	Major changes and new opportunities	164
13	Many moves and much activity	179
14	Relationships new and old	199
15	Beside the seaside, beside the sea	218
16	Back in the beautiful Blue Mountains	243
17	An unexpected new chapter in my life	267
Epilogue		275

FOREWORD

My intention is to live in the present, yet here I am, reviewing my eighty-four years of life and revisiting the past. It's been an unexpectedly worthwhile experience, and it's one I would recommend to anyone. Looking at past events has given me a new perspective, and the ability to see things from the point of view of the other 'characters' in my life story. I have felt great compassion for them.

I was surprised when writing, to find how inaccurate some of my memories were. Stories I'd often recounted, differed from what I'd written about them at the time. So I'm very aware that my memories of events are just that—my memories of my experiences.

* * *

Since I completed the first draft of this book the world has completely changed. In Australia, in late 2019, serious drought conditions led many of us to 'Buy a Bale' (of hay) to help our farmers survive. We would see photos on Facebook of truck after truck loaded with hay, driving into outback areas. Then followed the most serious and widespread bushfires this country has ever known—

FOREWORD

and our entertainers (and performers worldwide) came together and raised millions of dollars to help those made homeless, the charities supporting them, and the volunteer firefighters who risked (and often lost) their lives. Many of us joined in worldwide prayers for rain—gentle, consistent rain. And it came. There was some flooding, but most of the brown, bare land became green again.

Then out of the blue, a new variety of coronavirus began spreading COVID-19 to just about every country in the world. At present there is no vaccine for this virus, and no-one knows what the future will bring. People throughout the world are now living in social isolation. Where I live, we can be fined or imprisoned if we fail to abide by the regulations. Apart from those we live with, we must stay 1.5 metres away from any other person, and public gatherings are limited to two people. We are to stay at home unless doing necessary shopping, receiving medical care, exercising (once a day, no stopping) or travelling to work or education (if they can't be done at home). No sitting in a park or lying on a beach. Playgrounds are roped off. No-one can freely enter or leave the country or travel interstate. Many countries are in lockdown.

This pandemic has closed down businesses, schools, universities, all public performances, cinemas and sporting events. Cafes and restaurants can only provide take-away food. It's predicted that 3.4 million Australians will lose their jobs. Many are able to work from home, but businesses are folding. It's now about six weeks since our self-isolation began, and it's not known if it will continue for another month, or several months, or even a year.

JUST AN ORDINARY PERSON

I'm very much aware of the numbers of people who are suffering or fearful. My heart goes out to them. I've joined some of the new Facebook prayer groups, and am spending more time in prayer and meditation, and feeling love and gratitude as I visualise everyone living in health and harmony, and the planet lush and productive—the air fresh, the oceans clean and clear.

COVID-19 has forced us to look at life differently, to reassess our priorities and find new and better ways of doing things. People are cooperating and opening their hearts to one another, and acts of kindness are escalating. Thanks to technology and the internet, most of us can still connect, be informed, be entertained, do our shopping, and continue our education. My young grandchildren have video lessons sent from their school, and I'm using Zoom to give them piano lessons online. (There have been numerous excellent webinars on using technology for distance teaching.) The world's greatest musicians and entertainers are using Facebook to come into our homes daily; operas, musicals, concerts, and Shakespeare plays can all be viewed and enjoyed, mostly for free, at present. Leading speakers, thinkers, and 'celebrities' are also offering a great deal of support. And all are full of gratitude for the selfless work of the many doctors and nurses caring for the vast numbers of ill and dying patients and bereaved families.

I'm very fortunate that I live alone, am happy with my own company, have all I need, and am fairly 'tech-savvy'. Many older people don't have the ability to arrange for home deliveries or access the internet. Many families have several generations sharing a small living room, as they are together 24/7. Many are bored—sales

FOREWORD

of alcohol and chocolate have skyrocketed—but so have sales of musical instruments and gym equipment.

Some people believe this pandemic is a wake-up call for humanity—an opportunity to make major changes in the way we treat one another and our planet. I share that view. This seems to me to be part of a major evolutionary change, the beginning of what has, in the past, been described as 'Heaven on Earth'—a time when all of us will act from a place of inner wisdom and love.

CHAPTER 1

ON BEING A MOTHER

I always wanted to be a mother. When I was a little girl and people asked me what I wanted to be when I grew up, my answer was always 'I want to be a mother'. I was born in Australia in 1935, a time when it was rare for women to go out to work. They would maybe get a job between leaving school or university and finding a husband, but the goal and expectation of most girls was marriage and domestic duties. When I married at age twenty-two, a few months after graduating from Sydney University and when still living with my parents, we decided twelve children would be nice—whatever came along. But none came along. Month after month I would be hopeful, only to have those hopes dashed.

Hindsight can reveal patterns in our life experiences, and looking back over my own long life I am aware that the dominant storylines have all, in their own way, centred on motherhood. After initially struggling with infertility, I adopted two children and fostered two more before eventually giving birth to three. My mothering experiences with these seven much-loved souls presented me with the greatest joys and the greatest challenges of my life.

Interestingly, even beyond my own children I have found myself drawn again and again to 'mothering' roles—from teaching students in the classroom and in private piano lessons, to leading village youth clubs, to organising a youth theatre group, to caring for the elderly and infirm. There were also step-children and children that I minded or baby-sat from time to time.

I have long believed in re-incarnation, and the theory that 'all the world's a stage' and we are each playing our assigned and pre-agreed roles. In this particular life it would appear that I've been well and truly typecast in the role of mother.

CHAPTER 2

MY FAMILY OF ORIGIN

My mother, Colina Kinlock Spicer, was born in 1908. She was an only child. There'd been a stillborn baby before her, and another stillborn after her.

'My mother is a Maori', I told my friends when I was very young; and I believed it at the time. I knew that New Zealand's Maoris had dark skin and hair. My mother was olive-skinned, had very dark hair, hazel eyes and had been born in New Zealand, so I thought I was right. But the truth was that her mother had travelled from their home in Victoria, Australia, to the Christchurch clinic of the famous Dr Truby King for the birth.

My mother's mother, Mary Flora Campbell, was a highly educated woman who married 'beneath her' to William Walter Spicer, a piano player and a photographer who liked to keep bees. The Campbell family were proud of their lineage as they were descendants of the Duke and Duchess of Argyle—though my grandmother,

MY FAMILY OF ORIGIN

like her husband, had been born in Victoria, Australia. My mother told me that her mother had run a very high-class residential establishment in Melbourne, where haute cuisine meals prepared by the students were served to the public at lunchtime on weekdays. Etiquette was everything—as it was with my mother. I've recently read, in an old press cutting, that my grandmother was a noted French scholar, and for many years was the Director of the Melbourne blind institute. Knowing she married a man outside her social class who played the piano at blind institutes, I presume that's where she met my grandfather. The Royal Victorian Institute for the Blind, which was in operation from 1866 to 2004, provided accommodation, education and training for 120 adults and children with hearing and sight disabilities. It was the first such institute in Australia.

My mother's father spent many years as a peripatetic musician, entertaining inmates of prisons and lunatic asylums (hospitals for the mentally ill) as well as institutes for the blind. When at home, he donned his beekeeper's hat and attended to his beloved bees. He served in the 1914 - 1918 World War and received a medal for distinguished service. His service, however, was playing piano in the Officers' Mess. He never left the country.

When my mother was fourteen, she and her parents moved to Sydney. At that time, the school standards and syllabuses in Victoria and New South Wales were so different that she left school soon after arrival in Sydney, and began tertiary studies at Sydney's Conservatorium of Music. Having already been studying dramatic art with Madame Locking in Melbourne, she now became a student of

JUST AN ORDINARY PERSON

Mr Lawrence Campbell. I remember her telling me about his insistence on physical exercises and good posture. A few years later, when she went to a man who claimed to 'make anyone two inches taller or you'd get your money back', she was informed that he could do nothing for her, as her posture couldn't be improved upon.

I believe my mother was the youngest person to receive a teaching diploma in dramatic art and singing when she graduated. But, in those days, it was considered prudent for girls to have secretarial skills, so she also learned shorthand and typing and became a journalist, writing for a women's magazine. In her spare time she ran her own amateur theatre company and gave private elocution and singing lessons.

I never knew my mother's mother, as she died some years before my birth. But my mother's father, who we called Granddaddy, I loved dearly and saw regularly. He lived near us, and visited every Thursday until his death when I was eight. Each week as I arrived home from school I'd hear him playing Scott Joplin and other 'non-classical' pieces on the piano as I walked down the side path to our front door. I loved it. After the evening meal we always played cards or Tiddlywinks with him before going to bed. He then played the best two-out-of-three games of euchre with my mother before walking to his home—the caretaker's cottage in Parramatta Park. We often visited him there, and spent many happy hours in the park with the emus to look at and the cannon guns to climb on. Being a photographer, he took lots of photographs of us—some in the park, some at home—with camera on tripod, and a large black cloth over his head to keep the light out of the camera.

MY FAMILY OF ORIGIN

At that time, Mr Spicer (as he was known to everybody else—even my father and my father's parents called him that) was no longer playing piano professionally. He worked at the Parramatta School of Arts, where he ran the lending library and took bookings from ballet and tap dance teachers for the hire of the rooms. I think he was the only employee there, apart from the cleaners. On my parents' wedding certificate, he is described as 'Librarian, The Park, Parramatta'.

'Grandaddy is eccentric' is how my mother described him to us. She explained what eccentric meant. Looking back I can see that his weekly attendance at séances (for which he borrowed our wind-up His Master's Voice record player), his photography of ectoplasm, and his views on food-combining, better sight without glasses, and natural health were quite unusual for the time. But he did enjoy excellent health. And it never deteriorated.

One day, when he was seventy and still working full-time, he took the train to Sydney to attend to some business and to have my watch repaired. As usual, he visited the Sanitarium Health Food Store for his lunch. He sat down, placed his order, leaned his head against the wall, and died! Two ladies who knew my grandfather came into the shop.

'Oh! There's Mr Spicer! Let's go over and say hello to him', said one.

'Looks like he's nodded off', her friend replied.

JUST AN ORDINARY PERSON

What was sad about Grandaddy's death was the fact that someone phoned my mother and told her he'd 'had an accident'. She spent a distressing twenty-four hours calling hospitals trying to track him down, worrying about his injuries. She was actually relieved to eventually learn that he had died peacefully and been taken to the morgue. I don't recall any of my family being upset by or fearful of death, but I do remember my mother saying that the people we loved lived on forever in our minds and in our hearts.

* * *

My father's parents May (nee Powell) and Edmund Yates Lynam (Ted) lived even closer to us as I was growing up. We lived at numbers 19 then 21, and they were at number 22 in Lansdowne St., Parramatta. I called them Namma and Grandpa, and I loved being with them and staying overnight at their house. He would do mental arithmetic with me. She taught me the alphabet backwards and how to spell 'mosquito', among other words. They had all the National Geographic magazines, a pianola with lots of paper rolls and a clock that chimed every fifteen minutes twenty-four hours a day. I loved sleeping in their living room and listening to the different chimes. When I was very young my grandmother had a music studio and taught eleven instruments from premises above one of Parramatta's picture theatres. Her lifelong hobby was gardening. Whenever possible, she was out in the garden at dawn every day, all year round.

Several times I went away with them during school holidays. I have very fond memories of long, early-morning walks on the

MY FAMILY OF ORIGIN

beach with my grandfather when staying at a holiday house belonging to friends of my parents, on the bay side of Palm Beach. Afterwards we would stand near the pier and watch the fishermen gutting and cleaning their catch. Back at the house we'd read and talk about horse racing—a lifelong interest of his, but one not shared by his wife. I loved reading the 'form' of each of the horses running the next Saturday. These were the days of Bernborough, and only a few years after Phar Lap—two of Australia's super horses.

My grandfather was a 'self-made' man. Born in Yorkshire, England, he came to Australia with his family when he was a baby. His was a family of architects, surveyors and educationalists. He, however, had little formal education.

'When I turned twelve I had to leave school to support Granny' (his mother) he told me. 'My first job was delivering coal.'

I know that he also worked on the tramways in Sydney. But for many years after that, he and my grandmother worked long hours together in shops they owned. Some of them were newsagents, some gift shops, some general stores, but for every one of them my grandparents made and served homemade cordials, chocolates and ice cream. His ice cream and fruit drinks won first prize in the Royal Easter Show in Sydney one year, and as more and more shopkeepers wanted to buy from him, my grandfather and his youngest son Reg ended up full-time ice cream manufacturers. Their factory was behind the family house in Parramatta. Their company, E.Y. & R. Lynam, became Lynam's Ice Cream Pty Ltd, later amalgamated with Streets, and later still was bought out by

Unilever, leaving my grandparents and uncle quite wealthy. In their final ten years together my grandparents were able to travel to Europe and Asia, and thoroughly enjoy their retirement.

I grew up believing my grandfather's father had died before the family left England and came to live in Australia. But recently I was given a number of birth, death and marriage documents relating to his mother—my great grandmother, Emily Lynam. Known to everyone as Granny Lynam, Emily lived in the country town of Wingello, and only visited Sydney occasionally. She came to Parramatta when I was a baby, and I'm in possession of a lovely photo in which four generations of us are sitting on a bench in my grandfather's backyard. My father is holding me, his father is sitting beside him and Granny Lynam is next in line. As a child I met her a few times before she died at ninety-six when I was just seven. I remember a sweet little old woman, dressed completely in black, sitting in a rocking chair, knitting. But what a life she'd had, according to the documents.

The first of her twelve children had been born when she was nineteen—just six months after marrying. By 1879, when she left Yorkshire and came to Australia by ship, she'd given birth to another six, of which my grandfather was the youngest. It seems number eight arrived as soon as the boat docked in Melbourne. The three oldest children, aged eleven, ten and nine, remained in England! My great grandmother later had twins who died soon after birth, another son and another daughter. The ones who stayed in England later visited, and two of them settled here.

MY FAMILY OF ORIGIN

Granny Lynam's husband, while shown on census forms as a surveyor and civil engineer, enjoyed his drink and just 'lived the life of a gentleman'. The family in England actually arranged and paid for the passage to Australia in order to get rid of him, and they regularly sent money directly to her until her death more than sixty years later. According to one document, she opened a dressmaking establishment in Sydney to help support the family. Her husband remained a 'gentleman' until his death at fifty. I now understand why my grandfather, the oldest son living with them, came to join the workforce as a twelve-year-old.

My father's mother, May, also had many siblings, though several of them didn't reach adulthood. My childhood memories include numerous visits to five of her siblings and six of Grandpa's. I had lots of great aunts and great uncles and second cousins, but was sad that I had no first cousins.

My grandmother had one sibling who 'we don't mention'. I once I googled my grandparents' names and found, among other things, a Sydney Morning Herald notice dated 9 September 1922. My grandmother's 'unmentioned' sister and husband had taken them to court for £182.10 they claimed they were owed; at the time the couple were running a business owned by my grandparents, and presumably that dispute was the reason for the permanent rift.

A few years ago I was given some old family documents and artefacts, and was surprised to find several letters to my grandmother in an ancient and musty small leather wallet. The letters dated back to the 1880s, and most were still with their envelopes.

JUST AN ORDINARY PERSON

Along with letters from her father and various aunts, I was astonished and moved emotionally by one of them. It was a letter my grandfather had written to my grandmother soon after their marriage. He may have been uneducated and made many mistakes in spelling and punctuation, but there was no mistaking his feelings, his regrets, his hope, his love for her.

Believing she regretted the marriage, and without discussing it with her or saying goodbye, my grandfather had gone to Africa to serve in the Boer War (1899-1902) as a Light Horseman. She'd written a number of letters to him, but he'd previously felt unable to reply. In this letter, dated Oct 20th, 1901, and written from Klerksdorp, South Africa, he mentioned the heat, the sickness and the deaths of people they both knew, then referred to her latest letter to him where she said she was staying in Katoomba and had never enjoyed herself so much in her life. I quote some excerpts, his original spelling and wording intact:

I am not Enjoying my self nor did I come here for Enjoyment My Dear. Now you ask me once again why I came here and why I left you for 12 months.

I fancied you were sorry you had promised me to marry me so I made up my mind That I would not ruin your Life but I would go away. And this was the only place I thought of first. I wish to God I Had made up my mind to go somewhere Else and then I could of stoped. But as it was I Had signed on thinking I was Doing you more good than Harm. I knew I was ruining my own Life.

MY FAMILY OF ORIGIN

I tell you this May as sure as their is a God Above me and I Hope I never see Xmas if I am telling a Lie. I was going to see you the Last night if I Had Died through it to say good By. But I do not think I would of Explained it to you so you know now Love I am very sorry to say I misswronged you.'

'Both of us Have been Punished Enough by our foolishness I think what is the matter with us is that we do not tell one another our troubles ……… So let us be more outspoken to one another in the future and tell our troubles and thoughts to one another and then things will be more satisfactory. Don't you think so Love. I am very sorry to hear it is raining so much ………'

He signs off with

I remain Your

Ever Loving Husband

till Death parts us

E. Y. Lynam

xxxxx for your own

Dear self

I still feel quite emotional reading these words and experiencing a part of my grandparents' life I'd been completely unaware of.

JUST AN ORDINARY PERSON

Three years after the Boer War ended, my father, Walter Beaumont Lynam, was born. Reg, his only sibling, arrived four years later. My grandparents' marriage of fifty-six years ended with my grandfather's death in 1957.

* * *

'My Daddy is a funny Daddy. He has orange hair and glasses.'

This was my first composition at school. By 'funny', I was referring to the fact that my father was such fun to be with—whether rolling on the floor with us when we were very young, 'making music' at the meal table by tapping his spoon on glasses and glass dishes, telling us fantastic bedtime stories (off the top of his head) or responding to situations with wonderfully witty remarks. He was the best teller of jokes I've ever encountered; they were always clean, clever and quietly delivered. My father was never the life of the party, but everyone loved him and enjoyed being with him. He had empathy. He was very wise. He was calm. People came to him with problems and always went away empowered to solve them themselves. He never lent money, but helped many with their financial difficulties. He never bought anything—house, car, small items—until he'd saved enough money to buy them outright. I was in my mid-teens when he bought his first car. All possible savings went into the bank (at fifteen percent interest) and investments in properties.

MY FAMILY OF ORIGIN

My father had been a sickly child. Like his father, formal education ended at age twelve. What was in those days called a 'nervous breakdown' caused him to leave the prestigious Fort St Boys' High School in Sydney. However, he was able to continue his musical studies at the Sydney Conservatorium, and he educated himself by reading extensively. Although the family moved to Katoomba in the Blue Mountains west of Sydney, presumably for the fresh mountain air, throughout his teenage years my father travelled to the city by train for his lessons in piano, clarinet and composition. He had the amazing ability to learn from memory, on the train, a completely new piece of music.

In Katoomba, he conducted the local orchestra (his mother was its leading violinist) and helped with his family's shop. He did some of the pyrography, or hot poker work, on their wooden souvenirs/gifts. He also played piano accompaniments for many local singers and instrumentalists. And, like his mother, he was a keen gardener.

When he met my mother, he was living with his parents above their shop in Parramatta. Having completed his studies, he was now a qualified piano teacher and a published composer, as Walter B Lynam. In Parramatta my father wrote and produced and number of musicals, dramatic shows and comedy sketches. A few famous people got their acting starts in those shows. Chips Rafferty was one of them. We knew him as John—and this was in the days when children didn't call adults by their Christian names. His full name was John William Pilbean Goffage. He was a comedian in a double act my father wrote for—*The Long and the Short of It*. John was very tall; his onstage partner, Tommy Chalmers, very short. (We knew Tommy well, too. He later worked at the family's ice cream factory.)

John became Chips Rafferty and began his film career when I was five, but he continued to be a close friend, and regularly visited us for a meal and conversation when we lived in Parramatta. We loved hearing about his films and the people he was meeting. He told us all about visiting the Queen and the young Princesses Elizabeth and Margaret Rose in London.

I was so happy sitting in our lounge room after we'd eaten, listening to all of his exciting stories. And wow! When he said, 'You look so much like the princesses', I think I grew a few inches. One of the music books I loved was a beautifully illustrated edition of Fraser Simpson's settings of A.A. Milne verses. It was dedicated to the Royal Princesses. We used to sing those songs most nights as we gathered around the piano. Elizabeth was nine years older than me. Margaret Rose just five years older. I loved hearing about them. At that time my other 'role model' was the child actress Shirley Temple, also older by five years. She had her own little house and furniture all scaled to her size. What a dream situation.

My parents had met when my mother joined the cast, as leading lady, of one of my father's productions. During the years that followed, he proposed marriage a number of times, but she'd made up her mind not to marry until thirty. Maybe she feared losing him, but whatever the reason, she was just twenty-six and he twenty-

MY FAMILY OF ORIGIN

eight when they had their simple ceremony on 25 April 1934 (Anzac Day in Australia, a national holiday). The date was chosen so they'd always be able to spend that day together. After their wedding in Sydney, they caught a train to Stanwell Tops (between Sydney and Wollongong) and spent a weekend there before moving in with his parents above their Parramatta shop.

They married during what was known as the Great Depression, which lasted from 1930 to 1939 in Australia. Following America's Wall St crash of 1929, an ecomonic depression rapidly spread worldwide. Australia borrowed vast sums of money from overseas banks as income from our exports fell, local industries came to a standstill and unemployment rapidly increased. In the struggle to pay its debts, the government cut wages and pensions, and increased taxation. Many people lost their jobs, their investments and their savings.

My mother and father started life together with nothing. When her father offered a honeymoon or a lounge suite, they chose the furniture. Being a journalist, actress and later a top radio announcer, my mother was for many years the main breadwinner in our family. My father's income from piano teaching and composing would not have gone far.

Their plan was to work and save, then travel Australia for a year before starting a family. They did work, and they did save—they were both outstanding at money management—but their plans to travel were very much hit on the head when, less than four months into the marriage, my mother conceived me.

JUST AN ORDINARY PERSON

Her pregnancy was a difficult one, and she ended up suffering severe toxaemia and oedema. Her new doctor had presumed she was naturally 'big', and hadn't recognised the symptoms. My birth was traumatic, horrific, and ended with the attending doctor phoning my father and telling him,

'Neither mother nor baby is expected to live'.

My mother had had no idea what childbirth entailed. Before marrying, she'd read a book her father left on the table for her to look at. It gave basic information on 'the birds and the bees'. Her only preparation for giving birth was the advice given by a well-meaning aunt, who told her,

'As soon as you feel pain, ask the doctor for a needle. When you wake up it will all be over'.

Because of her bad state of health my mother was sent to a small naturopathic hospital a few days before my birth. After three days of 'fasting' (she recalled the occasional cracker thinly spread with Vegemite but no butter; she loved butter), she went into labour and at the first pain told the nurse she was ready for the needle.

'We don't do things that way here, Mrs Lynam!' was the response.

According to my mother, the pain was so bad that she screamed and screamed until she eventually lost consciousness. And the doctor in attendance, who just happened to be an expert in

MY FAMILY OF ORIGIN

medieval French, recognised that while unconscious she was speaking in that language. And she'd never learned any French in this life!

It doesn't surprise me that after coming into the world like that, I refused to feed from my mother. But I was in an establishment where they did things naturally, and the doctor believed I'd eventually feed if not given a substitute. After ten days of water and glucose the nurses defied the doctor's orders and gave me formula. We both survived, but I never did breastfeed.

Looking back, I feel great compassion for my mother. The pregnancy was unplanned and not wanted at that time. She'd given up smoking, having been told it could harm the baby. She'd had most of her teeth removed and replaced by dentures and a partial plate. Before my birth she'd been extremely ill for weeks. She'd had a devastating labour. And, at the end of it all, I was not the *red-headed boy* she expected.

From the beginning, my parents had been absolutely certain they were having a boy. He would have wavy red hair, and would be named Derek. They were completely thrown when I arrived. Their baby was a girl with very, very short blonde hair. (My mother used to say that at twelve-months-old my fair hair was still no longer than the hair on an arm, and everybody thought I was a boy.)

The nurses at the hospital called me Estralita, but my parents just couldn't come up with a name for me. Some six weeks later, on the last day possible to register my birth, they made up their minds. My father's most recent musical composition had been a successful one. It was an operetta set in Algiers, and was named after its French/Algerian heroine, Diane (French pronunciation). They decided to call me Diane. For my middle name, they chose my maternal grandmother's maiden name of Campbell.

CHAPTER 3

AH YES, I REMEMBER IT WELL

Before I was born, my parents made the decision to never disagree or use bad language in front of their children. I have absolutely no memories of any disharmony between them, and, as to swear words, I doubt they ever used them. From my mother I heard 'golly' and 'gosh' a few times, and maybe a 'crikey' once or twice. But I had absolutely no models for handling conflict, and no exposure to the so-called negative emotions. I was never aware of any disagreement, argument, fear or regret. I never heard a raised voice.

My mother did everything to the highest standard. She was always elegantly dressed and beautifully groomed. She really was extraordinarily talented. She was an excellent cook, and I doubt that any chef could cut onions or parsley as finely as she did. She could prepare delicious and nutritious meals 'on a shoestring'. My father grew many of our fruits and vegetables. I recall the spinach leaves and stems being served as two vegetables on our plates, and chokos prepared 'three-ways' at times. As a dessert, the chokos were cooked in a light syrup with a few drops of cochineal; they looked and tasted like stewed quinces. My mother served very healthy food—she didn't peel potatoes until after they'd been cooked; she didn't ever peel the carrots or parsnips. We had small helpings of everything. Unless we were entertaining we usually had fruit for dessert, sometimes accompanied by junket, blancmange or Spanish Cream—a kind of whipped jelly. Cakes were only baked at Christmastime, on birthdays and for visitors. But those cakes and the desserts for visitors were something I'll never forget. Our professional-looking, rich, fruit-and-nut-filled Christmas cake was always covered in marzipan, then royal icing, and topped with a sprig of holly. The luscious chocolate cakes with chocolate icing would often be smothered in beautifully arranged, freshly blanched almonds. The memory of our upside-down banana caramel puddings is something that makes my mouth water still.

In those days smoking was considered most elegant, and my mother enjoyed up to five filter-tipped cigarettes a day. I disliked the smell and vowed I'd never smoke, while my sister, eleven months younger than me, couldn't wait to grow up and become a smoker.

My sister was named Colina (my mother's name), but I called her 'Tina', and as there were many Colinas in my mother's family, she was called Tina at home. She and I always had a daily supplement of a spoonful of cod-liver oil (followed by half an orange to suck on, to take away the taste). Castor oil was given for the occasional constipation (again with the half orange), and for common colds we inhaled Friar's Balsam with a towel over our heads and had Vicks VapoRub soothingly applied to our chests in bed at night. Like most people at the time, we had the contagious diseases of measles, whooping cough and mumps. But, in general, we were very healthy and active children.

Among my mother's skills was dressmaking. She made beautiful clothes for herself and for us. I remember how stunning she looked in a magnificent strapless ballgown she designed and made on her Singer sewing machine. But I also recall the fact that she was always running late with her sewing. As teenagers, we were invariably sewn into our new dresses when we first wore them; the zippers had never been added in time. We would be cut out of the dress when we got home.

When we were very young, my mother attended evening classes in child psychology because she wanted to do the best job possible of parenting us. Her teacher was the famous Dr Morven Brown. He had attended school in Parramatta and lived in the area.

I remember both of my parents regularly attending local adult education classes for the next twenty-five years or so—until my father's death. In these classes, usually held in the home of one of the members, they studied the classics, the arts and many other subjects. My father was an avid reader all his life. His IQ was in the genius range and he loved learning. They both enjoyed good books, discussions and meeting new people. However, I suspect the decision for my mother to study child psychology was triggered by an incident when I was just twelve months old. It was immediately after Tina was born.

While my mother was in hospital, my grandmother had looked after me and rocked me to sleep each night, a boiled lolly in my mouth. On discharge from hospital, our little family of four went away for two weeks to have some time together—I think it was to a friend's flat near Sydney's Bondi Beach. Not surprisingly, I cried loudly and persistently when put to bed (in one of their suitcases) with no rocking and no sweet. Out of consideration for the people in the adjoining flat, I was nursed until I fell asleep. But once home, my mother decided this had to stop.

The first night, after being put in my cot, I screamed and screamed. My grandmother was there, and she became most upset and said I must be picked up and comforted. She said I could become hysterical and harm myself if left. So I was picked up. But the very next morning my mother went off to the clinic for advice. She was informed that I could not hurt myself if left to cry.

That night I was put down and left. By the time I'd exhausted myself crying and had fallen asleep, my grandmother had walked out, announcing she was severing all ties with her daughter-in-law. I think it was a couple of weeks before they spoke again and harmony was restored. Fortunately for my parents, the very next night when I was put to bed I settled and went to sleep without a murmur. I don't think I remember any of this happening—I was just under twelve months old—but it was an event my mother never forgot.

AH YES, I REMEMBER IT WELL

And when I was told about it, it became significant to me, too. (And I've relived it in therapy.)

My earliest conscious memories are of when I was just two, and living at number 19 Lansdowne St., Parramatta. Counsellors claim that the earliest memory has great significance. The first incident I recall was one that was repeated a number of times. I was sitting on the toilet seat waiting for my mother. As usual I'd called out, 'Mummy or Daddy, I'm finished!' I can still hear my singsongy voice signalling to them I was ready to have my bottom wiped. My mother always called back, 'I'll be there in a minute, Sweetie'. I had already formed a concept of what a minute was, and when it was always so much longer than that before my mother arrived, I came to the conclusion that there was something very wrong with me. I wouldn't have dreamed of speaking about it. My parents were perfect beings in my eyes. No, I was definitely at fault. In fact, I was thirty-five when I came to realise my mother wasn't perfect. And I never did go through any teenage 'rebellion' or time of not seeing eye-to-eye with my parents.

A little later, still aged two, I attended a kindergarten each weekday. Miss Glassen, who was in charge of that kindergarten in North Parramatta, picked me up from home in her car each morning and drove me back at the end of the day. I used to talk too much at lunchtime and not eat my lunch, so I had to eat alone. I remember feeling sad about that, as I found talking much more enjoyable than eating. Other strong memories were of the boy who ate snails from the kindergarten's garden, of accidentally breaking my thermos flask of hot soup, and of the large painted circles on the floor in the main room. The circles were perfect for our organised games, such as 'Drop the Hanky', but their main use was for our afternoon sleep. Every day, after lunch, we would form a circle before rolling up in a blanket on the floor.

Looking back I'm aware of what might be called 'psychic experiences' when I was very young. In bed at night, with my eyes shut, I would see a horse with a long horn coming out of its forehead. And sometimes I'd see an eye. When I first heard the term 'Eye of Horus' I knew that's what I'd seen, even though I had no idea at the time what it meant. And one day when helping clear the table after lunch, I decided to smell the pepper in the pepper pot. It filled my eyes and I had to have a bandage wrapped around my head, covering my closed eyes. I then exclaimed,

'There's a man with a banana in his ear!' My parents looked out through the window and saw a man walking down the footpath opposite our house with an ear trumpet in his ear.

Something memorable for another reason happened one Christmas day when I was three or four. In our earliest years, my sister and I were not only dressed identically but all our bought clothes were boy's clothes. My mother said they were better made and more suitable for play. It was probably true, but maybe she hadn't totally come to terms with not having a son. Anyway, one December morning I met up with other children in the street, and we showed each other what we'd got from Santa.

'I got pyjamas and a raincoat', I proudly declared.

AH YES, I REMEMBER IT WELL

The others looked at the boy's pyjamas and the raincoat, which buttoned up on the boy's side.

'You're a boy!' was their response. I was thrown. I'd always thought I was a girl. I went home quite upset and asked, 'Mummy, am I a boy or a girl?' Of course, she reassured me I was a girl. However, I've often wished I was male. I've always had difficulty choosing feminine clothing, and have frequently thought how much easier and more comfortable dressing would be if I were a man.

* * *

At four I started school. My father had taught himself bookkeeping and was now running the office at the ice cream factory where his father and brother did the practical work and his uncle Fred drove the delivery truck. My mother had moved from journalism to radio announcing.

I googled my mother's name recently, and was amazed to immediately see a professional photograph of her taken in the early 1940s. And there was a newspaper article from 1942 giving details of a Parramatta concert I'd actually attended and remembered. The headline reads: 'RADIO STAR IN CONCERT' [The event] 'will give admirers of Colina Lynam, radio star of 2UE, an opportunity of seeing and meeting this popular artist, who will appear in a sketch'. Amazingly, I recently came across the words of that sketch—it's one that most visitors to our house requested. My father was always asked to play piano pieces, and my mother to sing and to perform 'The Serial Story'. Her typed copy of it was among her papers when she died, and it's now in my possession, along with the Order of Australia medal and certificate she received in 1979 for service to the community.

When my mother was at 2UE, radio announcers did much more than announcing. She wrote scripts for all kinds of programs. She wrote and delivered advertisements. She performed in radio plays. And she compered a weekly afternoon audience show called *Get Together*, where she sang, asked quiz questions and gave out cash prizes.

I found another newspaper article from that era which mentioned a change of venue for this show due to 'the increasing demand from listeners to take part in the session'. A colleague and close friend of hers, Sid Everett, joined my mother for these Thursday-afternoon events. He had a beautiful, deep bass voice, and I still remember his renditions of 'Short'nin' Bread' and 'Ol' Man River'.

An interesting thing about Sid and his wife was that they had a baby without realising it! They were Christian Scientists. She hadn't seen a doctor. She was aware that she'd put on some weight, but didn't put two and two together. Others were aware of the pregnancy, especially when she 'threw up' when they were all out sailing together. But no one realised the parents-to-be were oblivious to the fact.

During the first World War, many goods were rationed, as they were in short supply. We had coupons for clothes, butter, sugar and tea. Everyone had a ration book—even children from five years of age. A clothing coupon book had 112 coupons for twelve months. A man's suit required about thirty-eight coupons. A boy's shirt required five. The Everetts hadn't saved any clothing coupons, and obviously hadn't bought anything for their new baby. On the day their son was born, my mother had to collect clothing coupons to add to her own, then dash off and buy some essential clothes and wraps to take to the hospital for their baby.

Sid and his wife were good friends of our family. Other 2UE colleagues I got to know were 'Scrim' (Gary Scrimgeour), Alan Toohey, Tal Ordell, Bill (Honey) Honeyfield, Gwen Plumb, and the General Manager, 'Paddy' Campbell-Jones.

During the war, my mother created a radio segment where she read letters to an imaginary soldier serving overseas. The listeners became so emotionally involved that several of them actually sent items to be included in packages for him. Some listeners became family friends, and Tina and I often accompanied our mother on visits to their homes.

During school holidays we'd usually spend one day 'going to work' with her. We'd get a train to Wynyard and walk up to the Bligh Street studios in Savoy House and say hello to everyone there. Then Tina and I would be taken back down to ground level in the big and ornate metal lift and go into the Savoy Theatre, where we'd see a film. My mother would then always take us to lunch at Cahill's restaurant—ending with ice cream cake and their famous caramel sauce.

JUST AN ORDINARY PERSON

When the war ended, Colina Lynam was the only announcer in the 2UE studios. She became the first woman in Australia to read the news.

* * *

Our family moved house a lot when I was young. Our first house, number 19, was on a double block. By the time I was five, my father had bought a kit house, which he and a handyman friend turned into a beautiful fibro residence at number 21. A fence was erected between the two, and our old house was then let to a family on a rent-and-buy basis, so they eventually became its owners.

I lived at number 21 for a total of nine years, and I remember it well. Just before we moved in, my father painted our new bedroom walls a 'Lolly Pink' colour. The colour was intense, and I recall that he had a number of bilious attacks while applying the paint. When it was finished and the paint had dried, it was obvious to everyone that the walls would have to be repainted in another colour. It took many coats of cream paint to cover those deep pink walls. But that bedroom, which I shared with Tina, became the loveliest room. On every wall there were framed illustrated verses from *A Child's Garden of Verse*. The pictures were beautifully drawn and coloured, and the words were in large letters that could be read while lying in bed.

Once the lights were out at night, Tina and I had many conversations about which one of us was going to marry Johnny, the boy next door at number 23. His kitchen window was opposite our bedroom window, and we'd often fall asleep listening to the exciting wrestling matches his grandfather liked to listen to on their kitchen radio. I rather enjoyed the gruesome descriptions of toe-twisting, etc. Johnny had a crystal set radio, which we sometimes listened to at his place. But usually, he spent his free time at our place.

Johnny was an only child. His grandparents lived with him and his parents. When his grandmother died, it was my first experience of death. As soon as we were told, Tina and I went off and had a fit of the giggles. I knew people weren't supposed to react like that, and it was comforting for me to be with someone who responded the same way.

When I was little, with my parents or in public, I was always trying to be grown up. I was quite a serious little girl, never playing with dolls or toys or doing what I considered 'childish' things. But when alone with my sister, I could be myself. I remember a time when we both picked our noses, had a farting competition and laughed our heads off. Tina was my best friend. She boosted my self-confidence. She always looked up to me, figuratively speaking. Physically, she reached my height when she was three, and after that was literally looking down on me. But she was completely unconditional in her love and admiration of me.

Although we were quite different in our abilities and interests, Tina repeated many of my 'patterns' throughout her fifty-two years of life. At primary school, she too skipped a class and repeated a

JUST AN ORDINARY PERSON

class. After leaving high school, she too re-sat the Leaving Certificate exam, studying at the same coaching college before going to Sydney University on a Commonwealth Scholarship—all one year after I did. Tina got a part-time job selling bread and cakes at David Jones some time after I started there, while we were both at uni. She married after I did, and had her first baby nine months after I adopted my first child. And we both married twice.

* * *

When we were young and at home during the day, we spent a lot of time outside. We would play with our friends or just sit in our favourite tree, sometimes picking its mulberries or its leaves for silkworms but often just 'being'. Whether with friends or just my sister, I was always the one who decided what was to be done, and I then allocated the jobs. I would bake a cake and get all the kudos. Tina would have gone off to the shop for me for eggs or whatever, and she would have done much of the work, but never even got an honourable mention. With the local children, I remember organising a gardening project when I was quite young. We would grow vegetables and sell them to the parents. I had them all digging, marking rows, sewing seeds and watering. I just told everyone what to do.

When my mother was at home, we both helped her with baking and preparing meals, setting the table and washing up. I used to feel honoured to be allowed to dust the pianos—my father's grand, and my upright one. And I remember the enjoyment of cleaning the beautiful, big brass trays, which served as occasional tables. Sweeping was probably my favourite activity—and it's something that still brings me pleasure. I feel great when my surroundings are freshly cleaned and attractive. I've always loved 'housework'. I see it as a non-demanding and enjoyable way of changing things for the better.

Growing up, I compared myself to my 'amazingly talented parents' and believed I had no hope of ever being a patch on them. I decided then and there that working on a conveyor belt, like the women in the ice cream factory, would be a good match for me. I occasionally helped out there in school holidays, folding cartons for the ice cream 'bricks'.

All my family were great readers, except me. I rarely read a book, as I wanted to do things. My main reading materials of choice were books of information and books of proverbs. I actually made a scrapbook with wise old sayings, such as 'A stitch in time saves nine' and 'Don't put all your eggs in one basket'. I was particularly intrigued by the contradictory ones 'Look before you leap' and 'He who hesitates is lost'. But my favourite was 'The proof of the pudding is in the eating'. For that one I added a beautiful coloured illustration of a big round Christmas pudding. Maybe my mother was an influence here. She was forever saying 'First things first', 'Never put off till tomorrow what you can do today', 'If a job's worth doing, it's worth doing well', and 'If you can't say anything good about a person, don't say anything at all'. She read us many of Hilaire Belloc's 'Cautionary Tales' as a way of teaching us how to behave.

JUST AN ORDINARY PERSON

We'd just got settled nicely into our second house, number 19, when my family moved again. Our new house was at Glenbrook in the Blue Mountains west of Sydney. World War II was escalating, and a few months before midget Japanese submarines appeared in Sydney Harbour my parents decided to move away from the city for safety. A couple of months after we went to Glenbrook, a reporter from Radio Pictorial of Australia did a feature article for that magazine. Some of those pages are among the many newspaper clippings now in my possession. In the issue dated 1 March 1942, a photo of my mother, Tina and me is featured on the cover. The interview itself has provided me with some details and information I'd not known before—though it quotes my mother when talking about the very early starts to her working days, as saying:

'I don't know whether my husband brings me a cup of tea in bed or whether I just dream he does!'

My mother never, ever drank tea. It was cups of coffee my father took in to wake her up every morning. We used to sometimes tease her and pretend she'd had a coffee, when she hadn't. She was oblivious. She would be lying flat on her back, coffee cup balanced on her chest. I don't recall one ever being spilt. Sometimes she would drink two or three cups of black coffee before waking to normal consciousness.

According to the article, we moved to Glenbrook on Christmas Day 1941. Houses were scarce, and my mother had 'hiked miles—from Springwood to Valley Heights, to Warimoo, to

AH YES, I REMEMBER IT WELL

Blaxland, to Glenbrook—before she found "SunnyBrae" ... in order that the youngsters would be safely removed from the terrors of any possible air-raids.' The article mentions that some Glenbrook residents had to buy their water. I hadn't known that. I do remember that we had a well in addition to tanks. And I remember clearly the live-in housekeeper, who introduced us to the word 'sin', when we jumped over one of my father's garden beds. And I'll never forget how she pulled out our loose teeth by tying string around them, attaching the other end to the door knob, then firmly closing the door.

There was no sewerage at our Glenbrook home. We had an outside toilet a long way from the house in the backyard. The 'night soil man' regularly removed the metal pan from under its wooden seat, replacing it with a clean one, before sealing it with a lid and taking it away. He did this through an opening at the back. Our access was through the full-sized front door. We always needed to watch out for venomous spiders when we went to the toilet. And we were not allowed to enter the unused garage because of snakes.

Meat, butter and perishable foodstuffs were hung in mesh-covered containers on our southern-side verandah, where the shade and breeze kept them fresh. In Parramatta, we'd not only had an instantaneous gas heater for the separate shower and bath, but we'd had an ice chest to keep food cold; the ice man came regularly in his horse and cart, and delivered enormous clocks of ice (he also provided manure for the garden, as my father would go out with a shovel after the horse had passed by).

JUST AN ORDINARY PERSON

At Glenbrook, the people opposite us had an enormous underground concrete air-raid shelter. And at school, we had to practise jumping under the desk or table. All overhead aeroplanes were treated with suspicion, but Tina and I had no fear of a Japanese invasion. Quite the opposite. Our mother had told us that she had lots of flour, sugar and other foodstuffs in the pantry, and that 'if the Japanese come, I will make them cakes and scones'. I was quite hoping they'd come, as cakes were a rarity in our household—and my mother's cakes were delicious works of art.

A very happy memory from that time is of the whole family sitting on the front verandah on hot summer evenings, our small legs dangling down, as we all enjoyed the local shop's lemonade ice-blocks. And I loved the weekend bush walks, where Tina and I clambered over so many beautiful rocks, first one to reach the top always declaring 'I'm the King of the Castle'.

However, three unhappy incidents stand out strongly. The first was a punishment by my mother for being naughty. I have no idea what I did to displease her. I always did my best to be good. Whatever it was, my punishment was not being allowed to attend a friend's birthday party—a penalty I felt was out of proportion to my 'crime'.

The second incident was one of my attempts to be an entrepreneur. My mother had lots of flags or badges—metal lapel pins that were sold regularly in the city as fundraisers for worthy organisations. She usually bought one each week, and they were never worn again. One sunny Sunday morning, Tina and I were up very early and I suggested we get some pocket money by selling these badges. We went door to door, sold them all (very cheaply) and with the proceeds we went to the local shop and bought chocolate- and coconut-covered marshmallow blocks, which we enjoyed eating while sitting on the swings in the park. But once we returned home and I proudly mentioned what we'd done, my mother's response was to accompany us to all the places where we'd sold the pins, return the money (it must have been provided by her), and tell the people that they could keep the badges. Disapproval was painful enough for me, but this was so humiliating. Also, it seemed quite wrong for the people to end up with both the pin and their money.

The third strong memory from my short time in Glenbrook was of playing the piano in a concert. At age six, I'd already done two piano exams, with my father as my teacher. The examiners had come to our house, so I'd played on my own piano. This was my first public performance, and I was to play a Brahms Waltz on stage in our school hall. (I think it was the only performing space in the area.) I wasn't the least bit nervous, and I knew the piece well. But I'd not played before on that piano, and I couldn't find my starting notes. I was used to getting my bearings from a small blemish on one of the keys on my piano at home. The headmaster, Mr Waterhouse, was standing just off stage, so he came on and showed me where to start. I played the first section. When it came time to repeat that music, I again needed to be shown the notes. There followed a contrasting section—and, yes, I again needed help for that. I carried on, quite unconcerned. What threw me was that when I next stopped, ready to return to the first (and last) section, the piece still unfinished, instead of showing me the notes the headmaster picked me up from the chair and carried me offstage. Performance ended. It was another six years before I would do another piano exam, and I never again played a solo in public. All my future performances were as an accompanist, where the limelight was on the person I was accompanying. 'My best isn't good enough' was what I told myself from that night on.

* * *

I was seven when we moved back to our newish home in Parramatta. A cousin of my father's had been renting it while we were in the mountains. I don't know why we left Glenbrook then. The Radio Pictorial article quotes my mother as saying, 'I think it will be many a Xmas before we move out, for we all adore living here'. The war hadn't ended. We still had blackout curtains and searchlights scanning the night sky. Maybe it was the early starts and long train travel both my parents were doing each weekday. But it may well have been because of the live-in housekeeper, whose outlook on life was so different from theirs. Anyway, after the move, I remember playing a Beethoven sonata when I auditioned and was accepted as a day girl (not a boarder) at Our Lady of Mercy College, Parramatta. For the next seven years, Tina and I caught the bus to and from that school, dressed in our brown uniforms, ties, hats and gloves. We were happy to be back in our lovely house opposite our grandparents again.

CHAPTER 4

SEVEN TO SEVENTEEN

I loved my seven years at OLMC. We'd gone to that school because of the music. And what wonderful musical opportunities we had! At age eight, I was thrilled when our choir travelled to a school close to Sydney, where we joined with other girls to sing an entire Mass in Gregorian chant. It was such a special and beautiful experience. I enjoyed everything we sang in our school choir, from 'The Road to the Isles' and Frank Hutchens' 'The Australian Sunrise' to songs written by a fellow student, pianist Pamela Page. And I still remember fondly being on stage at a school concert, dressed in costumes made from strips of blue, green and clear cellophane, swaying and singing, 'Little water sprites, all are we ... creatures of the wave, who love to brave the sea's eternal measures'. I'm always amazed at how music can take me back, and how much pleasure can keep coming from memories of happy times.

At OLMC there was the option of learning other instruments. Tina took up the violin. I tossed up between the harp and the cello;

JUST AN ORDINARY PERSON

I'd wanted to play the cello since the moment I first heard one on a record. So my parents bought me a child-size instrument, and I began cello lessons instead of Latin (my then favourite subject, but I had no option). I soon joined the school orchestra. I remember us playing in the Sydney Town Hall on one occasion—another happy and memorable event. OLMC recently posted on Facebook a 1945 photo of that orchestra, and I was astonished to see my ten-year-old self with my cello, and Tina with her violin, behind a cup we'd presumably won.

My father suffered from migraines and neuralgia all his adult life and was permanently on medication, but at one stage he became very seriously ill. The doctor was urgently called to our home, and said that, technically, my father had died. He then stated that either my father had to go away to recover, or Tina and I had to go somewhere else, as several weeks of complete rest was essential.

So for one term we became boarders at school, going home for weekends. One of the requirements for boarders was that they attend Mass at six o'clock every morning. Even though we were not Catholics, Tina and I were not excluded. However, Tina used to pretend to be asleep, and when the nuns came into the dormitory to check that everyone was up, they sometimes let her stay in bed. Of course, I was always the 'goody goody' who went to Mass. I remember how during the long midday prayers in our classroom, I would stay kneeling in the aisle long after the other girls had returned to their seats. In summer, perspiration would be streaming down my face, but I remained on my knees. The praise I got from the nuns was worth it. I was held up to the class as an example.

SEVEN TO SEVENTEEN

'And she's not even a Catholic!' they would point out, as I virtuously took my seat.

But when attending early morning Mass, having had the evening meal a good twelve hours earlier, I kept fainting. Actually, I was no stranger to fainting. While the women in my mother's family were strong and could deal with anything, my father and his mother readily fainted at bad news or unpleasant events. I recall the day my parents had been invited to go sailing with friends. My mother had turned on the iron to prepare a shirt for my father. He found an already ironed one. They dressed, took Tina and me across the road to our grandparents' house, and off they went. In those days, irons just got hotter and hotter if left on. My mother's iron burned right through the wooden ironing board, fell into a basket of our soft toys and began to burn the house down. There were four fire engines. I remember later that day seeing the pile of melted glass that had been our laundry window. Anyway, when my grandmother was phoned and given the news, she just keeled over, and had to be given 'smelling salts' to bring her round. Years later, when I was with my parents at a performance of *King Lear*, my father had to be helped up from the floor after the eye-gouging scene. He was empathic, compassionate and very aware of people's pain.

When I began fainting day after day in the school chapel and needed to be taken to the infirmary, Tina and I were told we could both sleep in and miss Mass. As I had the job of filling all the inkwells in our classroom, I'd often do that as soon as I was up and dressed and while the others were at the chapel. I was always a morning person. Tina made the most of her time in bed.

JUST AN ORDINARY PERSON

I liked being a boarder and welcomed the discipline; but Tina was homesick. I found it an interesting few months. On Saturday mornings one of the nuns would check our heads for lice, using a fine-tooth comb. We had baths with strict limits on the amount of water in the bath and the amount of time spent in the bath. The supervising nun would come in and check that we didn't have more than a few inches of water. And we had to be quick. In and out. We then dressed standing in front of our lockers, the little doors opened on both sides for privacy. It was a very small and restricted space and quite awkward.

From the time we'd moved back to Parramatta, we'd no longer needed a live-in housekeeper. My father's office was in his parents' house, in front of the ice cream factory and almost opposite us. We used to call in there so he could tie our ties before we caught the bus to school. My grandmother was the one who prepared our school lunches. I remember she used to bake us tiny rice, sago or tapioca milk puddings in individual-sized Pyrex dishes. We always went back to her place after school. I loved being there. I was happy playing the various piano rolls and singing along with them. There were all the old community songs like 'Let's All Go Down the Strand' and 'Pack Up Your Troubles'. Their gramophone records were different from ours, with lots of Peter Dawson songs, and 'Life on the Ocean Wave'. And they listened to the radio serials *Ada and Elsie* and *Dr Mac*, which I enjoyed whenever I stayed overnight.

Our home life was very happy. We always had a sing-song around the piano before bedtime. I enjoyed playing piano duets and two-piano pieces with my father, and I loved listening to him playing. He was an excellent pianist and had a large repertoire of all the classics. Beethoven, Chopin, Schumann, Schubert and Grieg were probably his favourites. My father also played as he composed, so I have happy memories of the sound of his piano concerto (which was later broadcast on the radio).

What I didn't like were my mother's theatrical performances. She was too good an actress for my comfort. She would turn into another person when she performed her dramatic monologue (the sketch), and I wished I could disappear through the floor. Was this my mother? I wondered. I was embarrassed and upset. Not only was I unsure which character my mother really was, I didn't like the limelight. I wanted to be inconspicuous. I recall walking on the opposite side of the road from my mother and Tina when returning from the train station one day, as I thought their lively conversation would attract attention and I didn't want to be a part of it.

My mother was often described as 'vivacious', and she had an energy and enthusiasm and warmth and spontaneity that others loved, but I hated. And at the pictures (cinema), she would get excited or laugh out loud—most embarrassing to someone who feels inadequate and doesn't want to be noticed. I cringe, however, when I remember one incident when we were on holiday and our family was eating together in a guest house dining room. I was the one who inadvertently brought attention to us all. I was asking my parents and Tina to speak more quietly when my fork slipped, and green peas went everywhere—over the table and onto the floor. I felt so ashamed of myself and was in a lot of pain. Looking now through adult eyes, it's almost unbelievable that a little girl would feel such anguish over an incident like that. But at the time, I truly wished to die.

My feelings of inadequacy had no doubt been strongly reinforced when the head of music at OLMC told me I was a child of the Devil. Sister was a talented musician who'd been a German countess 'in her own right' before joining the nunnery. I'd made a mistake when playing the piano in a lesson with her.

'Of course you will make mistakes, Diane. You can't help it. You are a child of the Devil because you haven't been baptised or christened. It's the Devil, not God, who is in you.' I don't remember feeling anything in response. But perhaps that was the main reason I baptised myself when I was eight.

At school I always treated religion like any other subject, and I always topped the class in it. But I found it confusing and contradictory. We were told that everyone had free will and could choose to do the right or wrong thing. We were also told about a book in which everything past, present and future had already been recorded. This concerned me greatly. I thought about it a lot.

It's now seventy-five years since I tried to make sense of such concepts. Just last week I read and reviewed a book that considers and addresses all these questions. Written by Pakistani-born American Rizwan Virk, its title is *The Simulation Hypothesis: An MIT Computer Scientist Shows Why Artificial Intelligence, Quantum Physics and Eastern Mystics All Agree We Are in a Video Game.*

SEVEN TO SEVENTEEN

Wow! This book opened my eyes to the possibility that our physical reality is part of a sophisticated, video game-like simulation where we all have multiple lives. Simulation Theory does explain some of the biggest mysteries of quantum and relativistic physics, and it fits in with long-held beliefs that we are living in some kind of illusion ('All the world's a stage'), and that there are other realities we can access with our minds.

But back to my childhood memories. I've never forgotten that when I was ten, I longed to have a baby brother or sister. I begged my mother to have another baby. When she said no, I told her that I would definitely have a baby when my daughter was ten. As it turned out, I gave birth to my first baby three months before my adopted daughter's tenth birthday. And she was absolutely wonderful with him, and with the two that followed.

World War II ended in 1945, when I was twelve. There were actually three endings: VE Day, 8 May (Victory in Europe Day), when the Nazis surrendered. Then VP Day, 15 August (Victory in the Pacific), the day Australians had a public holiday and celebrated Japan's agreement to surrender (made the previous day). And, finally, 2 September, the official ending, when Japan signed the unconditional surrender.

I remember that August day very well. We and the other children in our street went out onto the road with drums or whatever noise-producing things were available, while in Sydney, crowds of adults took to the street in spontaneous rejoicing. It was that congestion that prevented the 2UE newsreader from reaching the studio, and led to my mother announcing the end of the war. That night, we were permitted to have a sip of sherry as the family gathered around the radio to listen to the full news bulletin.

The end of the war meant food restrictions were off. Bacon, sugar, meat, fish, tea, jam, biscuits, breakfast cereals, cheese, eggs, milk and canned fruit had all officially been rationed. And rice had not been available. I remember the thrill of our first plate of rice with some tomato sauce stirred through, and a little grated cheese on top.

That Christmas, Tina and I were to get bicycles. This was a worry to my grandparents because of the trucks coming and going from their ice cream factory and from the soft-drinks factory directly opposite it. Grandpa offered us £10 each if we agreed not to ride a bike until we were sixteen. I took the money. Tina took the bike. I never did learn to ride properly, though I tried a few times. In my mid-fifties, after buying a new bike and making myself ride it every morning, I realised I didn't have to keep pushing myself to master cycling. I sold the bike and I haven't ridden since.

Swimming was a similar activity for me—something I came to dread. OLMC students all went to swimming classes at Granville. As a toddler, I'd been fearless in the water. But after a holiday with my grandmother at Manly Beach, when she wouldn't let us go into the water because of possible sharks, I'd become fearful. When I found myself in the pool at Granville, I refused to put my head under the water. Without any warning, the teacher pulled me under and held me down. I got such a shock; water went up my nose and down my throat and I was so uncomfortable and frightened. From then on I was allowed to stay out of the water, until the final day when I went into the pool and got a certificate for 'dog paddle'—but my feet never left the bottom and my head was well above water all the time I was 'swimming'.

I was fifteen and at the Conservatorium High School (the Con) when I next swam. This time our school class had gone by ferry to the Olympic Pool on the other side of Sydney Harbour. My best friend was an excellent swimmer—they even had a large pool at home. While she was doing impressive overarm lengthwise laps, I was nervously dog paddling, with the headmistress's right hand under my chin, and her left hand holding onto my swimsuit in the middle of my back. Day two, and every day after that, while on the ferry to the swimming class, my sight went. I just couldn't open my eyes. And so I was allowed to sit in the stands for the rest of the course. (Psychosomatic illness to the rescue again!)

A few years later, I did go swimming with friends, and I actually learned to dive and jump into the water from the poolside. After marrying I took free adult lessons, then private professional ones from a top coach, Forbes Carlisle. I developed some skills, but hated every minute of it. For hours beforehand I could hardly breathe; I was forcing myself to go into the pool. Eventually I stopped and stayed out of the water. But with each of my own children, I made sure they had happy experiences with water from a very early age, and all of them became good swimmers and enjoyed it.

JUST AN ORDINARY PERSON

Horse riding and tennis were different. OLMC had an excellent tennis coach, Vic Edwards. He later came to fame as coach and mentor of Evonne Goolagong, the Aboriginal girl who became Australia's number one player and won fourteen Grand Slams. Tina and I had weekly lessons at school, and when all the Catholic children were on retreat, we would spend the whole day on the court with Mr Edwards. Our surname was Lynam, and I can still hear him calling to us, 'Line 'm up and knock 'm down', as we lined up the balls in a special container.

The horse riding was not at school. On our rare holidays with our parents, we stayed at a quiet little guest house in the then-rural village of Wallacia, 68 kilometres west of Sydney. We children rode horses every day and danced in the converted barn-cum-ballroom to pianola rolls every evening. They didn't allow children under eight, but in those days children over eight were generally very well behaved and respective of their elders. The adults were able to have a most peaceful time reading, chatting, or just sitting outside enjoying the fresh, country air.

One year there was a retired British serviceman staying there. He was an early riser, and before breakfast every morning, all the children would join him in marching up and down the very long driveway between the road and the guesthouse. As we marched, military-style, we sang various songs he taught us. 'Slap dash, slap dash, up against the brick wall', is the one I remember best. We added hand movements in the appropriate places as we pretended to be applying whitewash to a wall.

SEVEN TO SEVENTEEN

These were such happy and carefree holidays. Every night we loved sliding around the ballroom's highly polished wooden floor as we danced The Gypsy Tap. And there was always the Pride of Erin, the Palais Glide, the Charleston and, appropriately, the Progressive Barn Dance. The pianola rolls included music from 'The Desert Song', and we'd sometimes be allowed into the ballroom during the day to play and sing those. We'd seen Max Oldaker on stage in that operetta, and knew all the songs from memory.

At home, when we had parties as young teenagers, my father would play 'The Dashing White Sergeant' on the piano as we danced Scottish quadrilles. We'd get him to go faster and faster. We also did square dancing, usually to a long-playing record that provided all the 'calls' for the choreography. And I recall another dance where we were in two long lines facing each other, and the music was the then-current pop song 'Silver Dollar'.

Many of our friends were Catholics, and when we had Saturday-night parties that went on into the early hours, we had to make sure we served supper in time for them to finish eating by midnight—as they needed to fast on Sunday until they'd taken Communion. My mother's suppers were delicious three-course meals!

A favourite party game of ours was dressing a partner using only sheets of newspaper and pins. The new outfits were put over the clothes being worn. Some of the boys were surprisingly good at this. I remember one outfit which included a handbag and hat as part of the ensemble. And some people made finely pleated skirts. All of our activities were creative and lots of fun.

JUST AN ORDINARY PERSON

I recall as a teenager going to a party at someone else's house, where all they played was 'Kiss in the Dark' and 'Truth or Dare'. For the first one, the girls sat on the lap of a boy (they were all strangers to me), the lights went out, then when the lights came back on, you were supposed to be kissing. Yuck! In 'Truth or Dare', described as 'the classic party game of embarrassment', you had to choose if you'd answer an embarrassing question truthfully or perform a 'dare', such as kissing someone or swearing. This kind of party had no attraction for me.

Throughout my teens I was rather innocent, naive, and not really interested in what we called 'the opposite sex'. My mother had taught us the facts of life from a very early age. In fact, at two, I corrected our housekeeper when she told me babies were found under cabbages.

'No', I said. 'Babies come from their mummies' tummies.' She was most disapproving of my mother's behaviour in telling us.

Our Catholic school had a specialist come and show us some anatomical drawings, and the nuns told us not to linger when washing certain parts of the body, and not to sleep with arms folded. It all meant nothing to me.

At sixteen, a second cousin gave me a pearl necklace for my birthday. I liked him, and knitted a navy jumper for when he did his National Service training (from 1951 - 1959 it was compulsory for 18-year-old men to undertake 176 days of military training). However, I didn't mind at all when my mother said I was too young to go to a public dance with him.

SEVEN TO SEVENTEEN

The nuns at school were not at all happy when my parents told them we were changing schools after I'd sat for the Intermediate Certificate, at age fourteen. In the seven years we'd been there they had failed to convert us, and we were leaving because of the musical opportunities at the Conservatorium. I felt more like a traitor than an ex-student then and for many years afterwards, but I'm happy to say that as an eighty-three-year-old I returned to OLMC for a special ex-students' reunion and was warmly welcomed. I enjoyed meeting and talking with others who'd had the same teachers, I joined them in a service in the same school chapel, and after lunch was taken to see their wonderfully equipped new music room.

* * *

Coinciding with our change in schools was another house move and our first car. My mother had given up her radio work, having been told it was better for teenagers to have a mother at home. She now worked from home as a freelance scriptwriter. I remember all her spiral-bound stenographer's notebooks where she wrote everything in shorthand before typing it up on her Remington typewriter.

Our new house was one that my parents designed and had built at Model Farms in the Hills District on the other side of Parramatta. It was the perfect family home for us. We had an ant-bed tennis court (Australia's professional 'clay courts' were built from ant-bed, loam and crushed granite), and a drive-in garage attached to a most beautiful and spacious house. There was a two-way wall between the kitchen and the dining room allowing our crockery and cutlery to be put in or taken out from either room; and there were floor-to-ceiling bookcases and a full-height, built-in cocktail cabinet in the living room. My parents rarely drank, but they always offered drinks to visitors. The local doctor had a sherry every time he called. In those days all GPs made house calls. If you were unwell you stayed in bed and the doctor visited. I don't remember ever attending a doctor's surgery.

We were very happy at Model Farms. Tina and I now had separate rooms. In our shared bedroom in Parramatta, I'd made an imaginary line to divide us, as she was carefree and untidy, and I was meticulous and liked everything 'just so'. In our new house there was even a spare room for visitors. Our school friends and pianists I was accompanying often came for the weekend to make music and play tennis with us.

My piano teacher at the Conservatorium, Lawrence Godfrey Smith, realised I'd never be a concert pianist but was a good accompanist, so he arranged for me to play with his more technically competent pupils in their concerto performances in eisteddfods and other competitions. At my lessons we spent a lot of time playing two-piano pieces and duets. He was a lovely man. I recall him giving me a beautiful potted plant one birthday.

Mr Smith had been my father's piano teacher. And Mr Smith's teacher, Leschetizky, had been taught by Czerny—one of Beethoven's most outstanding pupils. I've always liked that connection. As a piano teacher now, I'm aware of the special and close relationships often formed between teacher and pupil as they sit side-by-side week after week.

SEVEN TO SEVENTEEN

We travelled long hours to and from school at the Con. Tina and I would catch a bus to Parramatta, get the crowded train to Wynyard, then walk up to the other side of Macquarie Street, buying a sandwich lunch on the way. (I remember having a cheese and pineapple sandwich every day for months.)

At OLMC I had done well academically, reproducing word for word what I'd copied from the blackboard during lessons. That's what was expected of us, and we lost marks in exams if we changed even one word. There had been very strict discipline. The nuns made sure we did our homework and performed well in class. Standards were high. We always stood when spoken to, and had a great respect for our teachers. There was one lay teacher, however, and she always wore the same brooch on her lapel. Our class secretly bought her another brooch, which we wrapped and placed on her desk with a card saying 'Variety is the spice of life.'

The Con High School could not have been more different from OLMC. Inside our classroom it was often like St Trinian's. There were four girls in my class. No boys. But we shared the room with a slightly larger class, which included boys. On my first day there, when I stood to answer a maths question, the teacher threw a book at me. 'Don't be so stupid', she said.

Our French teacher nearly always left the classroom in tears, to be followed by the headmistress's arrival and a reminder that Miss Clark had won university medals for her French. Well, she may have been an outstanding French scholar, but she was unfortunate in her looks and in her ability to handle a class. Nora Clark was very thin, had extremely hairy arms and legs, a sharp nose and chin, and the most unflattering array of Shirley Temple curls, which bobbed and bounced wildly with each step she took. Some of the musically talented but badly behaved pupils in my classroom constantly taunted her.

- They set the classroom clock to ring its alarm mid-lesson

- They put sneezing powder on the blackboard duster, so that when she used it, she began sneezing uncontrollably

- And they read comics in class, and when told to hand them to her, they put the book inside the desk, sat on the lid and dared her to come and get it.

Miss Clark also taught us history—a subject new to me. I became excited and interested when I read a book of my father's about the period we were studying in class. But at the next lesson Miss Clark dismissed my contribution as having no validity—it wasn't in the textbook we were using. My interest in history never returned. I dropped the subject at the end of the year.

Surprisingly, when I was at the Con High School, there was no school choir or orchestra that my class could join. We fitted in tuition in musical history, form, theory, and our instrumental lessons, but our timetable was too full for anything else. At the time there was no choice in subjects until the final year, when we could drop one subject. I'd had to give up my favourites—Maths I and II and Chemistry—when I started there. And the only sport, apart from our initial visits to the Olympic Pool, was running around the building while our maths teacher stood at the door and watched us pass a couple of times. We would then all sit on the grass until the end of the period.

I do remember one other activity. I played Colonel Pickering in an excerpt from *Pygmalion* at an end-of-year school concert. With my hair slicked down with Brylcreem, a moustache and a man's suit and tie (and strongly resembling my mother's father), I delivered lines on stage for the first and last time.

In my two years at the Con High, I hardly did any homework. Most of the teachers weren't concerned. It was up to us. The headmistress said it was training for university. Well, it was, in a way. In those days most university students failed their first-year exams. I failed every one of my final-year school exams and then learned how to study unaided. I then did well in all my tertiary studies at university.

At the time of those Leaving Certificate exams I was overwhelmed. On one particular day I had three three-hour exams at two different venues in the city. One was in the morning, one in the afternoon and one at 5 pm, before the long trip home and more exams the next day. Even though I was awarded the maths prize at school because of my trial exam results, in the real exams I failed in every subject except oral French. Yes, I even failed in music. I'd done the usual Leaving Certificate piano exam two years earlier for my Intermediate Certificate, and had now chosen to do a more difficult internal exam, which included written counterpoint. Eugene

Goosens passed me in the practical component, but I got a 'post' (an offer to retake the exam) in the counterpoint paper, and the posts weren't held till the following year. Too late to count.

But I had no desire at that time for any further education. I had no interest at all in teaching, and university subjects had no appeal. My goal was marriage and motherhood. I remember looking up the exam results in the Sydney Morning Herald newspaper, but I didn't expect to pass, and I don't recall any feelings of disappointment.

And so it was decided that I would attend a residential 'finishing school' at Kirribilli on the northern side of Sydney Harbour, right on the water and almost under the famous bridge. The Memorial College of Household Arts and Sciences was its name. There, along with twelve other girls, I received professional instruction in cooking and dressmaking, along with non-professional instruction in dietetics and household management.

Unfortunately for us, the principal, the only residential staff member, was a woman who was divorced, had a daughter in a boarding school, and had no education or experience in Domestic Science. She had been an English teacher in a Domestic Science school. Her focus, apart from Shakespeare, was on women getting out of the house to go to charity events and do good deeds.

I was quite upset at the way the premises were run. There were fleas everywhere. We had to sprinkle flea powder on our bedding each day, and once a week we'd paint the bed frames with a special solution. And the cobwebs! I was appalled.

SEVEN TO SEVENTEEN

When our cooking teacher came each week she was usually disappointed and frustrated to discover that many of the ingredients she'd asked for were either missing or not fit to be used. If it was not essential, it was not bought. And the principal had an arrangement with the local greengrocer to buy 'dead ripe' produce at a reduced price. If we left over-ripe tomatoes, etc. on our plates, they, along with all other leftovers (including porridge) went into the stock pot that was always on the enormous fuel stove. Nothing was binned. There was no composting of food in those days, and we were made to eat the contents of the stock pot.

We did get to bake things, like neenish tarts and tiny butterfly sponge cakes for an Open Day. And we also made and served hot sausage rolls with home-made puff pastry—but we could hardly believe it when the principal would not allow us to serve tomato sauce with them, saying we'd already had our intake of vitamin C for the day.

Dietetics was one of the subjects she taught us, and I enjoyed it very much. We learned and memorised what vitamins and minerals were in various foods, and in what quantities, and what was needed for good health. Years later when I studied nutrition, I became aware that it's actually more important to understand how the body handles what we give it. For instance, eating something containing calcium does not mean the body uses that calcium. It's a complex subject, but fortunately, we don't need to study nutrition. In general, if foods are unprocessed and edible peels are left on, our bodies are able to absorb and assimilate all the nutrients.

JUST AN ORDINARY PERSON

Our physical exercise at the finishing school was mowing the steep slope that ran from the house to the water, using a hand-push lawn mower. The principal stressed the importance of working to 'perspiration point' each day, and this is how we did it. I was still having piano lessons at the Con, and was usually allowed to do piano practice while the others did the mowing. This is one thing I was happy about. But overall I was not happy there, though I do recall a fun evening when I went to a dance at the famous Trocadero with the other girls. We all wore evening dresses, and I was surprised when one of them stuffed her top with two hankies. We had 'blind dates' that night.

By mid-year I'd had enough, especially of the fleas, which always targeted me. I begged my mother to let me leave. Suddenly, going to university seemed a better option. I started thinking about retaking the Leaving Certificate and enrolling at Sydney University.

There was a serious consultation. My mother and the principal talked, while I waited nervously outside the door.

'She's like all the girls', said Mrs Moore. 'Just homesick, being away from home for the first time. I suggest you arrange for her to have a vocational guidance test. It will show she doesn't have the ability for university studies.' And she convinced my mother—which surprised and hurt me.

SEVEN TO SEVENTEEN

So I stayed at the school, but I took the test. My mother had persuaded me to say that my job of preference was hospital almonry. I didn't even know what the words meant, but I duly wrote them on the form before taking the tests. When the results and recommendations came there were three suggestions:

- An Arts/Law degree (I should start studying straight away to retake the LC in three months' time).

- High-class secretarial work (I had outstanding results in clerical numeracy and accuracy).

- Hospital almonry, 'in which you are keenly interested'.

Wow! My mother was on my side again, and I was allowed to leave the finishing school. My confidence had been given a boost, and I was ready to dedicate myself to study at a coaching college in the city. The teachers there were absolutely top class. I loved every bit of it as I rapidly worked through the syllabus in my various subjects. For oral French, I attended one-on-one lessons with a French woman at the Alliance Française. I remember that after my lesson we used to walk to the train together, speaking in French as we hurried along.

This time I got Honours in music, and As in all my other subjects. And I won a Commonwealth Scholarship to pay for my university tuition. The scholarship people told me, 'We've never before seen such a difference between two sets of results'.

JUST AN ORDINARY PERSON

I enrolled at the University of Sydney for year one of an Arts degree—my chosen subjects being Music, English, Psychology and Philosophy. But between then and the start of the academic year, we moved house yet again.

CHAPTER 5

TERTIARY STUDIES AND EXTRACURRICULAR ACTIVITIES

*H*ow devastating it must have been for my parents when after less than three years in our dream house, the decision was made to sell up and move in with my father's parents. Tina and I were told that Grandpa was very ill and in hospital, and he'd begged my father to live with him and Namma in a large, two-storey house he would buy at Blakehurst, south of Sydney. My father had been unable to refuse him.

My parents never expressed regret (not to us, anyway), but they must have been so disappointed. Tina and I took it in our stride. Our new house was very large and we still had separate rooms. A great-uncle who was a professional cabinet maker made us the most beautiful desks for our rooms. And I had a radio beside my bed. The classical music stations 2BL and 2FC closed down at ten o'clock each night and began transmission again at six in the mornings; I would go to sleep with the radio on, and be woken up by it next day. I loved that!

Our new house had a private sunroof on top with a high cement-rendered brick wall around it, so it was ideal for sun-baking in a swimsuit. (At that time, a natural tan was highly desirable.) An additional feature was the dishwashing machine—though my father used to say that whenever he wanted something, it was in the dishwasher either unwashed or waiting to be dried. In fact, Tina and I squabbled so much about who would rinse the plates and stack them in the machine and who would dry them and put them away, that I decided then and there that I would never have a dishwasher in any house of mine. And with all my moves and kitchen installations, I've never had one—though I am aware that today's models are more efficient than those of the 1950s.

My father's brother, our Uncle Reg, also moved to Blakehurst at around this time. By now, Lynam's Ice Cream had amalgamated with Streets Ice Cream. Grandpa and Uncle Reg were very well off—my father less so, as he'd been a shorter time in the business and had fewer shares.

Uncle Reg was an amateur movie maker. I remember seeing films he made of us when we were toddlers. His new house had its own cinema, and he and his wife did a lot of entertaining at home.

TERTIARY STUDIES AND EXTRACURRICULAR ACTIVITIES

I was there one night, watching *Lady Hamilton,* when my legs became incredibly itchy and I felt quite unwell. I was taken home early and was diagnosed with 'yellow jaundice'. On doctor's orders I spent the next six weeks in bed, and was not allowed any butter or fatty foods during that time. Fortunately, I was well enough to travel to Sydney University halfway through the orientation week that preceded the first term's classes.

Being enrolled in Music meant I was automatically in the department's Pro Musica choir and orchestra. But I also joined the Sydney University Musical Society, known as SUMS, a choir made up of students from all the departments as well as some members of the staff. All three groups had weekly rehearsals and put on concerts, so there was lots of enjoyable music making for me.

SUMS members could join with singers from other universities for an annual Intervarsity Choral Festival. These were held in the different states, so we would either travel, or we would billet visitors. At our Blakehurst home we were able to accommodate four interstate choristers when the venue was Sydney. Everyone would meet in the Great Hall at Sydney University, travel to a camp at Yarramundi for a week of rehearsals, then return to the city (where visitors would be billeted) for the days leading up to the Sydney Town Hall performance. I remember us being at Yarramundi and gathering in the dining hall to listen, on radio, to the Queen's coronation in 1953.

Unlike today's students, we didn't dress casually for classes. Girls always wore stockings with suspender belts or roll-ons (a foundation garment rolled on to the hips). We'd wear court shoes or dressy sandals, smart blouses tucked into belted skirts in summer, and twinsets with skirts in winter. Women didn't wear pants. I remember one of the girls had an eighteen-inch waist and always wore a very wide belt to emphasise it. After the war, with clothing material in full supply, the New Look had arrived, and skirts were very full with 'nipped in' waists.

The women's union, Manning House, was where my friends and I spent most of our time when not attending lectures. There we would sit and chat, discuss our assignments, and sometimes study and do homework, while drinking milkshakes. To my knowledge there was no alcohol available to uni students in the 1950s. (I was quite surprised when invited to speak at the University of Newcastle in 1993 to see students playing pool and drinking beer.) I always had my lunch at Manning House, choosing individual items from behind the glass cabinet. I remember there being a selection of baked vegetables, roast lamb and roast beef. Simple, home-cooked-style food.

But when studying, I was eating a lot. Before leaving home in the morning, I would cook and eat a very large steak, at least one fried egg, a fried banana and fried tomatoes. And after our family evening meal, when I went to my room to study, I would take with me mugs of cold soup. I'd open a can of condensed vegetable soup, add equal quantities of milk, stir it well, and then drink this as I worked at my desk. The weight went on. I was five foot four and I reached ten-and-a-half stone. I was most unhappy about the way I looked, and I'd stay home when the family went to visit relatives.

TERTIARY STUDIES AND EXTRACURRICULAR ACTIVITIES

So my mother contacted the doctor, and he prescribed Dexedrine. The tablets were to be taken before eight in the morning or they would prevent me from sleeping at night. Well, even taking them early, I found myself waking up at about 2 am each day, my mind racing and keen to study, but unable to reason accurately. However, in time, I got used to it.

One of the SUMS choir members was a skier. He and his friends from the CSIRO where he worked went to Mt. Perisher (near Mt Kosciuszko) every winter. I was invited to go with them in my first year, 1953. I very much enjoyed that holiday, learning to ski, and preparing meals and socialising in our small hut with these older, sophisticated people. I tasted beer for the first time, but didn't like it.

In my first-year exams I did well, winning the Frank Albert music prize and qualifying for the Music Honours course. At that time there was no degree course in music.

Partway through my second year at university, my parents made arrangements for Tina and me to have the following year off in order for us all to do a ten-month grand tour of Europe.

For extra pocket money for the trip, as I had no Friday lectures, I managed to get a Friday-morning job at Sydney's biggest department store, David Jones. There I sold cakes and, later, bread. I would change into my uniform, with my hair completely covered by a stiff white cap. I still remember my concern when first calculating where to cut the sixteen-pound slabs of fruit cake so the pieces would be the right size.

At the end of second year I again did well in the exams, as did Tina, who was by then studying Economics. I was given reading lists for my third-year subjects, and bought all the set books—all of James Joyce, Dickens and Thackeray, etc. Many of these I took with me on my travels.

My father got a bargain of a car from an Englishman who unexpectedly had to leave Australia. It was a beautiful, big leather-lined Austin Sheerline. He booked us, car and all, on a Danish freighter for the trip over to Europe, and on a big passenger liner for the trip back. The Automobile Association prepared detailed strip maps of the route my parents had carefully planned. We had books and books of these wonderful maps, showing road conditions and points of interest as well as which roads to take.

Travelling in our own car meant we were able to stay at little out-of-the-way villages, rather than tourist hotels, and we weren't tied to a particular timetable. I wanted to do some of the driving (my mother didn't drive and Tina was too young), so I got my license just before we set off. I remember the examiner making me promise to practise reverse parking before taking to the road, as in my test he'd had to take the wheel of the Sheerline as I tried to reverse into a narrow lane. My driving lessons had been in a much smaller car belonging to the driving school.

TERTIARY STUDIES AND EXTRACURRICULAR ACTIVITIES

Our ship was the 'Sumbawa', a twelve-passenger cargo ship belonging to the Danish East Asiatic Company. It sailed from Adelaide, so we began our trip with the drive from Sydney. The long straight roads were a great way for me to gain confidence and driving experience, though I did shudder when the first big road train overtook me.

We arrived in Adelaide in the middle of one of its worst heat waves. In the hotel, wet towels were hung from the open windows and we did little other than lie on our beds for a couple of days. But once we boarded the lovely 'Sumbawa', all was perfect.

The cabins were beautiful and so well appointed, with cedar chests of drawers, desks and bed frames. The food was out of this world, especially the freshly baked Danish pastries made for the passengers and crew for every morning and afternoon tea. On this trip there were only ten passengers, and we were four of them. The others were a young model, a nurse going to work in Denmark, a honeymoon couple and a middle-aged couple. The model taught Tina and me how to cleanse our faces and use makeup. The nurse needed to learn Danish in a hurry and was happy to have us join her for Danish lessons given by crew members.

I read my *Ulysses*, of course, and I got up early every morning to help the crew swab and scrub the deck. But Tina and I also spent quite a bit of time dancing around (more accurately 'sliding around') the slippery wooden rolling floor as the gramophone played the only records, 'Schwanda the Bagpiper' and 'The Moldau'. That was sixty-four years ago (when I was nineteen) but whenever I hear those pieces of music I'm still back on that boat, smelling its distinctive smell.

At exactly five o'clock every evening of the voyage, all the younger passengers met for cocktails, having first changed into our most glamorous clothes. We all drank what we called a 'gin and two'—equal parts gin, dry vermouth and sweet vermouth (with a maraschino cherry garnish)—before going to the dining room for a sumptuous evening meal. And so our five weeks passed.

My mother, though, didn't have a completely happy time. One night, in the dark, she tripped over the little metal strip between the cabin and the bathroom, and the chief officer had to put stitches in the gash in her chin. I realise, in retrospect, that my mother had a kind of saboteur preventing her from fully enjoying the good things in life. She was used to putting others first. Her life was one of hard work and service to others. So often, when she was about to be on the receiving end of a special treat, illness of some sort would 'arrive'.

The tour of Europe took us from Antwerp, our port of arrival, through Liechtenstein, Holland, France, Switzerland, Italy, Germany, Austria, Norway, Denmark, Sweden, England, Scotland and Wales, and then back again to the continent. We saw all the sights, visited all the great cathedrals and museums and art galleries, saw Errol Flynn playing roulette in the Monte Carlo casino, and Maria Callas performing at La Scala in Milan. We skied in Austria, met up with some of the 'Sumbawa' crew in Denmark, visited Stonehenge before it was fenced off, joined in the Cornish Floral Dance

TERTIARY STUDIES AND EXTRACURRICULAR ACTIVITIES

and attended the Chelsea Flower Show. In Florence, possibly my favourite city with its stunningly beautiful Duomo, my mother developed pleurisy and missed a wonderful performance of *Porgy and Bess*, which she'd been much looking forward to. On one of the unexpected extra days there, Tina and I were taken out on motorbikes by two rather amorous Italian men who were staying at our hotel. We learned and used the word 'basta' (enough).

Throughout our travels we usually had dinner, bed and breakfast at our overnight accommodation, and bought local bread, butter, fruit and cheese for our lunches. We were often the only overnight guests, and would sit and chat to our hosts as they prepared our evening meal.

We took lots of photographs, and had our rolls of negatives developed in the cities. My camera was a Kodak 'Brownie', and I ended up with dozens of tiny black-and-white photographs. I used a number of exercise books as travel diaries, every night recording my experiences and purchases.

Apart from butter melting on the floor of the car one day, the Sheerline was a lovely home from home, carrying our clothes and souvenirs and the four of us very comfortably, though it did break down in a tiny village in the north of Italy. The local mechanics were intrigued. They'd never seen a car like this. They were totally unfamiliar with English cars. They took the engine apart and spread all the bits on the garage floor like pieces of a jigsaw. My school French and their heavily accented French could have been completely different languages. In the end, they put the car pieces back as best they could, towed us to the top of a hill, and we rolled from the north of Italy to Venice, where more experienced and skillful mechanics put things to right.

By the time our trip was drawing to an end, my father learned that the large passenger liner we'd booked on could not take our car after all. The Danish East Asiatic Line had another cargo ship, which was about to leave Genoa for Australia, so we booked on that. But to our amazement, when we arrived at the port, the ship at the dock was 'Sumbawa'. It had replaced its 'sister', which was undergoing unexpected and urgent repairs. The same captain, the same chief officer and the same chief engineer greeted us with a 'welcome home!' We'd got to know them so well on the way over that it was lovely meeting up again for the five-week return trip, with the same delicious food, the same records to dance to, the same cocktails at five o'clock precisely and, with more of my novels to read, ready for my return to university.

* * *

Once we were back home, with several weeks before the start of the academic year, I took classes in shorthand and typing. And to my delight, I also undertook the job of chauffeur to my grandfather. Although still able to drive, he liked nothing better than relaxing in the back seat of his new semi-automatic Daimler as I drove him and my grandmother to visit relatives or take short holiday breaks. I was paid a set sum each week and my job included cleaning and checking the car before and after each use—regardless of the length of the trip. Being an extremely practical person, my grandfather knew the importance of regular maintenance and TLC of mechanical items, and he enjoyed spending his money this way.

He was basically a most frugal person, having worked hard and long hours all his life, and always investing any profits back into his business. But once he was financially well-off, he enjoyed placing bets on horses in the Saturday races. He'd always been interested in studying their form and following their progress, but now he could put some money on them once a week. He used a betting system, which he very strictly adhered to, and placed very small bets, usually £1. His enjoyment came from the whole process. He always came out on top, overall.

But it was necessary to go to the phone box at the end of the street to place those bets, as this hobby was not one he could share with his wife. Namma's father had been a drinker and gambler. According to her, prior to leaving his wife for another woman, he'd come home drunk every Friday night (payday) having already spent all his wages. My grandmother was strongly opposed to any form of gambling, and she did not approve of alcohol—though she always had a bottle of 'medicinal' brandy on her bedside table, and I remember an occasion in Blakehurst when she became quite merry after drinking a number of gin slings. She refused to believe there was gin in them (as she accepted her third glass), and thought my mother was teasing her when she said there was alcohol in the cocktails.

That summer, in my role as chauffeur, we travelled far and wide. We visited relatives on a large property near Mudgee, where

JUST AN ORDINARY PERSON

I rode a horse each day and learned to shoot rabbits. And we drove down the south coast of NSW, staying at motels.

Whenever eating out at a restaurant or hotel, my grandfather always ensured an excellent meal by bribing the chef. After ordering, he would tear a £10 note in half and hand one half to the waiter.

'This is for the chef', he would say. 'Tell him he gets the other half if I'm satisfied with my meal. I want a tender fillet steak, well done.' It never failed.

Once university resumed, Grandpa hired a professional chauffeur with uniform and all. But the man, though highly qualified, didn't last long.

Soon afterward my grandparents bought and moved into a small house a few doors away, and our family of four enjoyed more freedom. But my grandfather had further health problems, and didn't like being hospitalised. I recall him going to hospital once for a safe and simple procedure, and coming home with a most serious infection. So he employed a nurse to look after him at home when he was confined to bed with thrombosis. Eventually he had 24-hour home nursing. For several months Grandpa's brothers and sisters visited him, thinking each time that it would be their last visit.

I sailed through my final year studies, having read all the relevant books and articles prior to the lectures on them. That year, 1956, I played the piano for the deb's ball in the university's Great

TERTIARY STUDIES AND EXTRACURRICULAR ACTIVITIES

Hall. The glamorous debs and their partners danced in that magnificent (if freezing cold) hall, to my rendition of 'The Blue Danube Waltz'. I was also the pianist/accompanist for the University Revue that year—a demanding but wonderfully enjoyable experience. And in June, as usual, I attended the annual Intervarsity Choral Festival, again at Yarramundi, west of Sydney.

It was at Yarramundi that I met Tony. He was conducting the Melbourne University Choral Society, MUCS. Tony had already graduated in electrical engineering and was working for the PMG (Post Master General) Department in Melbourne. He was happy, confident and outgoing. He wore a most impressive knitted stocking cap (like a beanie attached to a very long scarf) and he wore the softest of jumpers. It was partly the feel of his jumper that melted my heart. After the camp and the concert, Tony drove his car back to Rye, on the Mornington Peninsula, where he lived with his parents. But we'd both been smitten. We'd exchanged addresses and we agreed to keep in touch by correspondence.

However, not long after he'd left I 'fell in love' with someone else. Since starting university, I'd been friendly with a member of SUMS who also lived in Blakehurst. He was a lecturer at Sydney University. His parents and my parents were members of a small adult education class that met at his place each week. He and I usually travelled home together—sometimes in the car my father had bought for me (and Tina) and sometimes using public transport, with a long walk from Hurstville Station. Like another of my best friends, he was unofficially engaged to a girl who, after graduating, had gone backpacking overseas for a year or two. We'd previously been like brother and sister, but now found we'd developed strong feelings for one another. I believed I was in love with him, and I wanted to be with him forever. He was torn, and said he would need time to think about it, and would then make a decision as to which one of us he would choose.

It was a tense and anxious three days for me before we were again driving home together.

'I've decided to do the right thing', he said. He'd chosen his 'fiancee'. I became quite hysterical in the car. My heart was broken, and there was no consoling me. I remember we sat in the car at the end of my street until I was collected enough to appear in front of my family.

He and I remained good friends, but when his fiancée returned they'd grown apart, and he ended up marrying someone else.

* * *

With the end of my BA degree course I was offered further scholarships—for either an Honours Degree in Music or a Diploma of Education, which would qualify me to teach in schools. I really wasn't interested in either, so my father suggested I get a job and earn some money, and I was most happy to do that. I applied to be an air hostess with Qantas, and was halfway through the interviews and studying for my First Aid Certificate when Tony and I met up again.

TERTIARY STUDIES AND EXTRACURRICULAR ACTIVITIES

We'd been corresponding by letter for six months and had got to know one another pretty well. (And I'd been carrying a tiny photo of him in the front of my little First Aid book.) Tony had driven to Sydney en route to a Brisbane wedding of mutual choir friends, and I joined him and two others for the car trip there and back.

I clearly remember the heat of that week! It was one of Australia's worst heat waves. The car, of course, had no air-conditioning. We drove with all windows open and towels on the seats under us. We stopped for milkshakes at numerous cafes along the way. I've experienced a week of forty-five-degree temperatures in Greece, but I've never felt hotter or more uncomfortable than I did on the day of that Queensland wedding—in my stockings and makeup.

On returning to Sydney, it was decided that I would go back to Victoria with Tony to meet his parents. I also made the decision to stop taking the Dexedrine tablets, and as a result I slept in the car for most of that long drive.

On my last day with Tony's family, the two of us travelled with a number of MUCS choir friends to Phillip Island. We sat together on a most beautiful beach while the others went off for a walk. Tony proposed to me there. And I most happily accepted.

The following day I flew back home. Ironically, for someone planning to be an air hostess, I was airsick and I ended up with an oxygen mask. But, being engaged, I was no longer eligible to work with any of the airlines. My Qantas application was withdrawn.

JUST AN ORDINARY PERSON

I applied for a couple of interesting jobs, but they involved training and wanted people long-term. So I ended up as a well-paid 'graduate clerical assistant' in the Taxation Department. It was an interesting and fortunately brief time of seeing first-hand how government departments work. After the war, the Australian government had employed returned servicemen, even if they were not fit for work. Some of our office staff just sat at their desks, sometimes head on desk, and did little or no work. That was preferable, though, to those who put the files in the wrong place. Our office was where all the triplicate taxation files were stored, and we were the ones who sent out final notices and 'letters of demand'. All the decisions were made in Canberra by people who had no idea of what was involved. (I've just remembered I signed a secrecy form—and had to swear on the Bible—so I'll not give further details.) Suffice it to say, it was frustrating but very easy work. The easiest way of earning money that I've ever experienced.

CHAPTER 6

MARRIAGE AND MOTHERHOOD

In June of 1957, Tony and I were married. He was keen to live in Sydney but was awaiting a transfer from Melbourne, so we began life together in a rented studio apartment in Toorak, Victoria. The main room had twin beds that disappeared into the wall under bookcases during the day, leaving plenty of room for entertaining. Our large and well-appointed kitchen had a fixed table and seating for four people. The bathroom and laundry were shared with one other person. Everything was in beautiful condition—in fact, the landlady was so concerned that our footwear didn't leave any shoe-polish marks on the kitchen linoleum, she insisted on 'shoes off' as we arrived at the top of the stairs.

JUST AN ORDINARY PERSON

Both Tony and a close friend of his who worked nearby came home for lunch each weekday. I spent most of my mornings preparing a delicious midday meal, then after lunch began work on a three-course evening meal. In my spare time I prepared elaborate dishes for weekend parties with friends. I remember a favourite recipe where there were about ten thin layers of cake, with filling between all the layers, and an apricot glazing over the top.

I loved all this cooking and entertaining, and I enjoyed singing and socialising with the Melbourne University graduate choir I'd joined. But as time went on, and there was no sign of any of the twelve children we'd planned to have, I decided to get a part-time job. From then until our move to Sydney (and for some time after it) I worked in market research for Balm Dulux/ICI. This involved interviewing people, and later designing questionnaires, and employing and training others. I learned to use a slide rule, and very much enjoyed the work. The interviews were about people's experiences painting their houses. I was usually invited inside, and sometimes offered refreshments, as I was shown and told about the rooms they had decorated.

When Tony got his transfer to Sydney we stayed at my parents' Blakehurst home until ours was built nearby at Miranda. With still no signs of pregnancy, I then visited a Macquarie St specialist, and Tony and I both underwent various tests and examinations. It was found that I had a retroverted womb, which supposedly reduced the chances of conceiving. Tony's sperm count was very low, and no normal sperm were sighted. We were told our chance of conceiving was about one in fifteen years. And so we applied for the

MARRIAGE AND MOTHERHOOD

adoption of a baby boy and a baby girl. We knew it would be several years before one would be available, so when the NSW Education Department advertised for untrained graduates to apply for high school teaching jobs (due to the shortage of trained teachers), I applied, as did Tina. With her Economics degree, she was asked to teach geography and history. I was recruited for music, and at my interview it was made clear that I was not to become pregnant. I told my gynaecologist at my next visit and asked about contraception.

'Do you want a baby or not?' he asked in disbelief. And he pointed out that if I did become pregnant while teaching, 'healthwise' I'd be fine and able to work until close to the birth.

I was surprised that the Education Department gave us no teacher training whatsoever, but fortunately I was able to spend time with a friend who was an experienced high school music teacher, and he gave me a number of lesson plans and lots of advice. And when I found I was to take a class of beginner violinists, I had a crash course from another friend who was a violin teacher.

I started off working part-time as a casual teacher at two different schools—Jannali and Penshurst. Jannali was a shock to the system! At the daily outdoor assemblies, the headmistress would criticise staff members. Discipline was nonexistent and morale was low. I was told that all the permanent teaching staff had applied for transfers, and that being 'casual' I should apply for full-time work at my other school. So after one term, I worked full-time at Penshurst Girls High where, in addition to teaching class music, I played the piano for the hymns at the daily assembly, and assisted the head of music with the school's productions of Gilbert and Sullivan operettas (which I also accompanied).

But on 7 December 1960 the Child Welfare Department informed us that a baby boy with a similar background to ours had been born the previous day, and we could bring him home from the hospital the following week. Over the weekend I painted the cane bassinet I'd bought earlier, and made sure everything else was ready.

And so, our little ray of sunshine we named Martin came into our lives. His adoption went through and we were the happiest of families. Of course, I notified the Education Department that I would not be returning to teaching in 1961.

Eighteen months later, the local child welfare officer asked us if we would take a state ward, an almost four-year-old boy who lived nearby and needed a new foster family. The child, Gordon, was officially classified as 'handicapped', but he was a healthy, bright and seemingly happy little boy with a hardly noticeable blemish on one side of his face. He'd been born with an extra 'ear', which had been removed soon after birth but had left him with one cheek slightly less chubby than the other. We officially became his foster parents in August 1962. The local child welfare officer told us that when Gordon was two (and the oldest of three children), his mother had been sent to gaol for obtaining money under false pretences; she'd bought a refrigerator on 'hire-purchase' and then sold it. His father (who himself had been a state ward) had left them. The three children had been placed with different families in different parts of the state of NSW. I was told that the couple who'd taken Gordon had hoped to keep him permanently as company for their biological son. When they learned that his mother hoped to have him back one day, they decided to give him up. They lived in the adjoining suburb to us, and so we'd been approached.

We told Gordon from the beginning that his biological mother loved him and wanted him back with her as soon as she was able to care for him, so when she asked to see him the following year, I took him to the department in Sydney to meet with her. While I was there, I mentioned to one of the staff that we were on their list for the adoption of a baby girl. And lo and behold, the following week we had a call to say our adopted daughter had been born.

Wendy was just eight days old when we brought her home. She was a very 'good' baby, but it soon became obvious that she was not responding to sound; she seemed to be deaf. The department asked if we wanted to return her! Neither of us would consider that for a moment. So tests with specialists were arranged. It was a lengthy process waiting for the necessary appointments, and by the time the tests were all over, Wendy was hearing normally.

But she had two left legs. Both legs and feet looked the same. So more tests were done and the diagnosis was a congenital hip disorder. We were told this could correct itself, and it did.

JUST AN ORDINARY PERSON

Wendy was about six months old when our family increased again. At twenty-eight and thirty-one years of age, we became foster parents to a fourteen-year-old girl.

At the time I was organist at the local church where Tony worshipped and conducted the choir. The minister had been asking for weeks if someone would give a home to a local state ward. He said her foster mother needed to go to England for spinal surgery, and he hoped she could be placed with another family and not have to be put in an institution. No one came forward, and time had run out, so we offered to take her—even though she was so much older than our other three.

Donna had been in and out of numerous foster families during her fourteen years of life. And she'd been known by many names, often taking on the surname of the family she joined. The unfortunate girl had never learned to use a knife and fork. With an undershot jaw, she had somewhat of a Neanderthal appearance. And due to a previously broken nose, she had difficulty breathing and was expected to need surgery. Her health was poor—she had never had a full week at school. Just the week before she came to us, she'd fallen off a climbing frame in the school's gymnasium. And she was in a special class for children of low IQ who were deemed not capable of coping with normal high school classes.

We learned that Donna's latest foster mother was *not* going abroad for surgery. That was an excuse to give up the girl, who was not what they'd hoped for. It seems the family's teenage son had gone off the rails and they feared their daughter would do the same.

MARRIAGE AND MOTHERHOOD

After seeing a TV program on fostering, they'd decided a foster daughter could be company for their fourteen-year-old.

But Donna and their daughter were like chalk and cheese, and they didn't like one another. They were the same age, but when I met them the biological daughter was looking very adult, dressed in stockings and court shoes and her hair 'up', while Donna wore bobby sox and lace-up shoes, a dowdy dress, and an unflattering pudding basin hairdo.

Once she was in our family, being loved and supported, Donna's transformation was amazing. One of the first changes was orthodontic work on her teeth and mouth to realign her jaw. We bought her nice clothes. My mother took her to the ballet in Sydney. Of course, she learned to eat with cutlery. But the most significant change was the change in her mental and physical health. Our local doctor had told me, 'She's just a sickly child. She'll always be like that.' But the owner of the local health food shop advised me to see a particular naturopath in Sydney.

'There's nothing to lose, and he might be able to help Donna', she said.

So we made an appointment and visited the naturopath. He didn't share the doctor's viewpoint at all. He was certain that Donna's breathing could become normal without surgery. We were offered two forms of treatment. The one we chose was four weeks of meals consisting of raw fruit, raw vegetables, nuts, dried fruits, seeds and eggs. (No dairy, meat, wheat or added sugar) Donna was also prescribed daily sunbaths in her swimsuit, before 10 am or after 2 pm. At the end of the four weeks, she was to have a three-day fast with bed rest—nothing to eat or drink except water if thirsty.

The difference in Donna was astounding. She was never unwell again. And at the end of the year, she did so well in school that she was moved to normal classes.

We were all blessed by this. During Donna's weeks of limited foods, we could hardly sit beside her eating our steaks! So we mostly followed a diet similar to hers, and we felt so well and full of energy that Tony and I had personal consultations with the naturopath, and we continued permanently to follow a mainly raw, non-dairy, vegetarian, whole-food diet. Local untreated goat's milk replaced the baby formula for Wendy.

Obviously, all of our family learned we'd become vegetarians, and they were aware of the difference our changed eating habits were making. Tina had for nine years suffered from an underactive thyroid. A Macquarie St specialist in Sydney had put her on medication when she was sixteen, and since then had tested her every six months, increasing the dosage every time. When I told her about the naturopath we'd visited, she wondered whether there was a natural way to help her thyroid function. I asked him about it, and he said 'yes'. So she too saw him and followed his advice to very gradually reduce her tablets while eating a whole-food, mostly raw vegetarian diet. By the time of her next visit to the specialist, Tina was totally off the medication, and her reading was normal for the first time. She then went on to astound her gynaecologist by having her

MARRIAGE AND MOTHERHOOD

second baby naturally—the first had ended up with an emergency caesarian. The doctor's view was 'Once a caesarian, always a caesarian'. He'd said that to her husband but not to her. He'd decided to pander to her wishes and act 'as if'. He really didn't believe a natural birth would be possible for her.

***

When children such as state wards are placed with new families, they usually behave 'perfectly' for some weeks, as they desperately want to be liked and loved and kept. They then show their true colours, or worse. 'Will you still love me if I'm naughty?'

We'd learned this when Gordon arrived. He was angelic, absolutely hiding any pain he'd experienced when taken from his previous foster parents and brother—to say nothing of the previous separation from his biological parents and siblings. Not yet four, hair slicked down and dressed in a bow tie, he was brought to the house of absolute strangers and told they were his new Mummy and Daddy. I do remember, though, his suggesting that 'Martin can go and live with Mrs Jones!', the neighbour.

With Donna, we again experienced weeks or maybe months of 'perfect' behaviour, followed by several instances of shoplifting with a school friend and extremely bad behaviour at home. And she had a large repertoire of swear words, which she didn't hesitate to use with us.

JUST AN ORDINARY PERSON

To my astonishment, my father, who like my mother had always had a great relationship with all four of our children, spoke to me in private one day.

'Dee, your three young ones have every chance of a happy and successful life. But Donna's behaviour and example could prevent that. She is too damaged already. I think you should give her up for the sake of the others.'

I couldn't believe it! How could I 'discard' a child like this? But I so much valued my father's viewpoint. He had more love and compassion than anyone I'd ever known. So Tony and I discussed it. We decided we would give her up, but would keep her and say nothing until such time as the department had found her another family home.

However, the department immediately told Donna, and the days that followed were extremely painful for all concerned as we waited for news of a placement. Naturally, Donna was angry and upset.

It was during this time of waiting that my father had a fatal stroke. He'd been in 'normal' health, and was up a ladder painting the ceiling of a property he owned at Cronulla. He and my mother were shortly to leave for an overseas trip, and he was preparing the unit for rental. I was phoned and asked to go there, as I lived ten minutes away. I found my father alone on the floor when I arrived, his head expanding like a red balloon with each heartbeat. He lost consciousness and his heart stopped, just before the ambulance arrived. They tried resuscitation, got him into the vehicle, and attached him to a machine. I sat in the front beside the driver as we headed for the nearest hospital. I remember so clearly how most of the cars on the road did not move over to let us pass, seemingly ignoring the screaming siren and forcing us to slow down, drive on the median strip, and weave in and out of the heavy traffic.

My father lasted another twenty-four hours at the hospital, but never regained consciousness. The machines kept him alive until then.

It was that first night—the night before he officially died—that, after an argument with me about time spent in the bathroom, Donna climbed out of her bedroom window and ran away. She was very fond of my father, and the news of his illness and my lack of thoughtfulness proved to be the breaking point for her.

It was some six days later that she was found, and taken into custody by the police while awaiting a court hearing. We were told she'd spent the first couple of days and nights on trains, and had met a young man who offered her accommodation with him. They'd had consensual intercourse. She was under age.

I had to attend the court hearing and publicly state that we were not willing to have Donna return to live with us. I hated myself for it, but the only emotion I recall feeling was my surprise and discomfort as the court typist loudly tapped out every word as I spoke. The courtroom, otherwise, was silent and strained and almost 'unreal'.

Donna was placed in a kind of boarding school for state wards. We visited as her parents with the other children every month until her schooling was finished. She was then enrolled in a dressmaking course (her choice) and placed with a couple who would provide accommodation and meals. She continued to pop in and see Tony at his work in the city when she went to the dentist for ongoing work. But in time, all contact was lost.

If there was one thing in my life I could change, it would be that decision not to keep Donna in our family. With hindsight, I believe my father 'couldn't live with himself' after suggesting it to me. Having learned—at the time of my first pregnancy—that my law-abiding mother chose to have an illegal abortion 'for the sake of Tina and me' when we were babies, I think she probably was responsible for my father's words to me about Donna.

*　*　*

During our years in Miranda, there was another incident I'll never forget. In my car driving home late one afternoon, the setting sun in my eyes, I ran over the four-year-old son of a neighbour and close friend. His house, a few doors before mine, had a sloping front yard and driveway. The gate to the road was open, and the boy's ball had rolled onto the road as I approached. I avoided the ball, and I avoided their dog that ran after the ball, but I didn't see the boy run onto the road after the dog until it was too late. I can still feel the

MARRIAGE AND MOTHERHOOD

sickening feeling as my car wheels ran over his body. But despite my distress, I was able to do what was necessary. His mother was beside herself, so I called the ambulance and her husband at work, and, after a quick dash home to my family, I spent the evening with her—at the hospital and at her home, where I prepared a meal for her other three children. That night we learned that apart from broken bones, the boy was concussed. It would not be until the next day that the extent of his injuries would be known.

The next morning we were told he was mentally fine, and the prognosis was the broken bones (all in the lower part of his body) would heal—an enormous relief. And it turned out that during the healing process, moving himself around using his arms, the little boy developed his upper body beautifully.

The day after that accident there was nothing I could do to help. Tony went to work. The boys went to school. It was my tennis day—I played each Friday with a group of women at the local courts. I decided I might as well go to tennis; it would take my mind off the accident. I was feeling a bit 'lost'. So I packed lunch for myself and Wendy, and spent the day at the courts.

The next day, however, I was surprised and saddened that word had got round the neighbourhood that I was hard-hearted and uncaring.

'How could she go and play tennis as if nothing had happened?'

JUST AN ORDINARY PERSON

I was hurt but, as usual, I didn't show my feelings or mention it to anyone. It just added to my feelings of inadequacy.

***

As our family had grown, we'd added a master bedroom and ensuite to our house. We thought about moving, and from time to time we seriously contemplated joining a community or starting a small community with like-minded friends. We'd got to know several families in our area who were all members of the Natural Health Society. We'd formed a local branch and regularly got together for picnics, recipe exchanges and book reviews. Some of us had travelled together to undertake an extensive course in 'natural health' and massage.

Eventually in 1966, Tony and I bought a block of land at Wahroonga, north of Sydney, and we chose an architect-designed Pettit and Sevitt house to be built on it. The block was narrow but deep—with bushland and a quarry at the back. The house was beautiful, with white painted brick walls, red cedar window frames and beams, and a covered verandah the full length of the house. There was a large 'rumpus room' with TV and children's toy boxes-cum-seats, and a very large living area which comfortably fitted the grand and upright pianos, our big 'modern' radiogram, floor to ceiling bookshelves, dining suite and lounge suite. The builders took longer than expected, and we had to move out of our Miranda home before the new one was finished. In fact, we ended up renting two houses before moving in.

MARRIAGE AND MOTHERHOOD

The day we left Miranda brought another memorable incident. We had talked with Gordon about the option of his using our surname when we moved to a different neighbourhood and different school. We'd all decided that it would be best. On moving day I was busy and ultra-efficient, but I hadn't realised what a big thing the coming changes would be for eight-year-old Gordon. While we were dealing with the removalists, the boys took off. Gordon had decided to run away and he'd persuaded six-year-old Martin to go with him. After we'd called the police, Tony and three-year-old Wendy went with the removalists to the house we'd rented while I stayed in our totally empty one, waiting and hoping for the boys to return. The parents of that little one I'd run over brought a mattress for me to sleep on, and a torch, as the electricity was disconnected. Thankfully, overnight the boys were returned. They'd travelled by train to Sydney's Central Station and had decided to sleep in the adjacent park. A middle-aged couple saw them and spoke to them (they identified themselves as Christians), and then drove them all the way back to our home in Miranda.

* * *

After that move, we enrolled the two boys in the school nearest our new house, and they seemed happy there. However, Gordon began stealing money while at school, and the headmistress advised us to take him to a counsellor in Sydney. This turned out to be of great benefit to him—and to me, as well, as I was required to spend time with one counsellor while Gordon had sessions with another. Through sand-play, painting and similar therapies, Gordon at last expressed his held-in anger, jealousy, loss. It took time, but it seemed to work.

Meanwhile, during my one-hour sessions, my eyes were opened! I saw myself, my mother and my relationship with her in a totally new light. I'd always thought how fortunate I was to have such a caring and supportive mother—especially before I was married, when she'd chosen my wedding ring and wedding dress, made all the arrangements for the ceremony and reception, and decided on the honeymoon venue. With Tony hundreds of miles away, it seemed to me at the time that my mother was being helpful. Now, sitting opposite this young but very professional therapist, I saw how quietly controlling my mother had always been. And not only with me—with just about everyone she encountered. Her gentle subtlety was amazing. I recalled how my father, on our European travels, would drive wearing a deer-stalker hat and with a pipe in his mouth. He didn't like the hat and he had never smoked, but nevertheless he did it to please my mother. She thought he looked most distinctive with these accoutrements, as he drove our impressive-looking motor car. (My father bore a strong resemblance to the British actor Lesley Howard, though I seem to remember it was Trevor Howard who always had a pipe in his mouth or hand.)

Some time after my sessions with the psychologist, I was shopping for a dress in Sydney's David Jones. My mother was with me, and I was undecided about two dresses. She strongly recommended one of them—and I suddenly realised her choice was the one that was the least flattering on me, and I bravely chose the other one. My mother made no comment.

MARRIAGE AND MOTHERHOOD

Once we were settled into our beautiful new house, life was very good. I was always aware, though, that Tony had me on a pedestal. He rarely voiced an opinion, and would leave all decisions up to me. I was so used to being told what to do by my mother, I sometimes wished he would take the initiative.

Back when we were living at Miranda, once I'd realised we were unlikely have the biological children we'd hoped for, we'd gone, most harmoniously, to a marriage guidance counsellor. I'd thought it best to seek professional help before any marital difficulties arose. We'd been given personality tests as well as counselling both separately and together. Our marriage was a good one. We loved one another, and wouldn't have dreamed of being unfaithful or not being together for life. However, much as I loved and enjoyed my family, I still felt inadequate and totally uncreative. I couldn't even create a new life—something that everyone else seemed to do so easily. Deep down I was sad and disappointed, but I tried not to show any emotions other than 'happy' ones.

In Wahroonga, as in Miranda, I was supplementing our income by doing part-time home demonstrations of Stanhome products. I'd started this in the hope that the training would improve my confidence. Even though I'd done some school teaching, I found speaking in front of adults daunting. My 'business' went well. The products were excellent and I was very happy telling people about them, doing demonstrations, leading some fun games, taking orders and booking further parties.

JUST AN ORDINARY PERSON

Since 1960 Tony and I had attended yoga classes. At first we'd taken Martin, when he was a baby, to a friend's place where he slept in a drawer while we went to our weekly class in the city. When we moved to Wahroonga we joined a yoga centre at St Ives, where all five of us took weekly classes. The teacher there was outstanding, and she introduced me to much more than physical yoga. I borrowed books from her library about reincarnation, astral travelling and 'walk-ins'. I read Rudolph Steiner and Lobsang Rampa, and became a 'Friend of Findhorn', the new spiritual community in Scotland being run by Peter and Eileen Caddy and their friend Dorothy Maclean. We subscribed to their mailing list for regular newsletters. By 1969. their 'exceptionally large vegetables' made the group world famous.

In addition to yoga lessons, our children were now all learning piano. Gordon was learning the violin, as well. They had tennis lessons, Wendy learned ballet, and much time was spent driving to and from activities of some kind. Tony and I continued to sing and socialise with the graduate choir and often held parties at home. Now that I had my father's grand piano as well as my upright one, I enjoyed playing two-piano music with a local pianist.

Tony was happy in his job, which required him to use a computer from time to time. This computer filled a large room in a building on the north side of the harbour, and had to be booked well in advance. I took a course in computer programming, which was being offered to women graduates of Sydney University. Apart

MARRIAGE AND MOTHERHOOD

from my monthly disappointment at not becoming pregnant, we were all extremely happy, healthy and content.

***

Tony was only thirty-seven, and I thirty-four, when his three months of long-service leave was due. He had signed up with the PMG department prior to beginning his university studies. We decided to travel with the children. We bought a secondhand VW Kombi and planned a 38,000-mile trip around and into the centre of Australia. The vehicle was perfect for us. The table and seats became a double bed, and with the roof raised there were two single beds up above, one on either side for Gordon and Martin. A hammock big enough for Wendy could be fitted above the front seats when the vehicle was stationary. There was a small stove, and enough room for our boxes of fresh food, Gordon's violin and music stand, the children's school books, and our clothes—not that we needed many. The van had no air-conditioning, and as we drove north, to the centre, to Darwin and around to Western Australia, we often travelled in our swimsuits. Whenever we saw clean water (in a pool or a trickling pipe for cattle), we'd get into or under it in order to cool ourselves and remove the red dust covering our skin.

It was a wonderful adventure for us all. We were rising with the sun, and going to bed when the sun went down. To me, that felt so perfect. We started our days outdoors, exercising. Then Gordon did his violin practice—also outdoors. Often there were cattle nearby, and the animals always came to the nearest fence, seemingly drawn by the music.

JUST AN ORDINARY PERSON

The van had no electricity, but we visited camping sites from time to time to wash our clothes and ourselves in hot water. I recall one very hot day when the moment I finished pegging our clothes on the line, I was able to start removing them. They'd completely dried in a few minutes.

In Uluru, then called Ayres Rock, Tony and I climbed to the very top. Nowadays, out of respect for the indigenous people, this is no longer a normal occurrence. (In fact, since writing this, the climb has been banned.) When we were there, there were few other travellers and no development at all.

Most of our time was spent driving through 'undeveloped' parts of the country, and I came to view the built-up areas in a new light. As we approached a town or city I was keenly aware of the electric lights, the buildings and the general infrastructure as having been added to the land. I found the development somewhat overpowering, and was always pleased to leave it behind and return to the natural beauty of the country.

During our travels we took the opportunity to meet up with friends and relatives in Armidale, Brisbane, Alice Springs, Perth, Adelaide, Melbourne and Canberra. The rough roads caused damage to the Kombi at times, and in Darwin we had to sleep at a motel, as our mobile home was hoisted up in the air being repaired. And in Melbourne we stayed with friends while a new axle was fitted.

MARRIAGE AND MOTHERHOOD

We were only stranded once, and that was in a very isolated spot in the far north of Queensland. The three children had a wonderful time searching the nearby area for things of interest. They found lots of animal bones, which they collected and arranged by the roadside. We had to wait until a passing vehicle appeared, then ask the driver to notify someone in the nearest 'town'. And eventually someone came and towed us to a place where makeshift repairs could be made.

How different it would be nowadays, with mobile phones and the internet. And how different would be the visual recording of our travels. We ended up with boxes and boxes of Kodachrome slides, which needed a projector and screen in order to be viewed. It was 'the thing' to invite friends for an evening of slides and supper.

Those Kodachrome boxes stayed with me for more than forty years. In 2016 I was sorting through everything prior to moving house, and when I opened the boxes I found the slides were completely covered in mould. I made the decision to throw them away. I'm now aware that mouldy slides can be cleaned and scanned but, as a result of my actions, we now have nothing but memories of that wonderful three-month adventure.

***

Once we were all home again, life resumed as before. But at a party, I met the headmaster of Epping Boys High School, and he suggested I join his music staff. Our three children were now at school, so I decided to return to teaching. At Epping I not only taught music, I was also asked to teach classes called Guidance. This subject included advice on studying—setting up the best environment and conditions for doing homework, and setting short-, medium- and long-term goals. But in these classes, any and every topic could be brought up. I recall one boy who'd read about plants having 'feelings'. This was a few years before the popular 1973 book 'The Secret Life of Plants', but I too had read about studies on plant behaviour, and the whole class became engaged in an interesting discussion on how plants can perceive and respond without eyes, ears or brains.

One night a week, three friends came to our house and we sang madrigals together. Marianne was one of them—the soprano. I'd known her since university days. She was a bit younger than me, and had been one of the first to do a degree in music rather than arts. Marianne was on the music staff at Abbotsleigh, a private girls' school just around the corner from where we lived. She suggested I apply for a job there.

I was interviewed and accepted by the then-headmistress, the well-known British educationalist and cricketer, Betty Archdale. I left Epping High at the end of the academic year and began teaching in Abbotsleigh's Junior School after the Christmas break. I was later moved to Abbotsleigh's Secondary School. It was such a joy teaching music (and some English) there. Every child was enthusiastic about singing and making music and most of them played instruments. The junior school had its own orchestra led by Jane Hazelwood, whose father was the leader of the Sydney Symphony Orchestra, and every class sang in three-part harmony. In the senior school, in addition to giving class lessons, I took the choir, and I had a number of students who were taking music as an examination subject. I drove the children to concerts in the school bus—after getting my truck driver's license—and I introduced them to 'modern' music, both in class activities and at public performances. It was a rich and fulfilling time.

In April 1971, Marianne told me about a conference being held in Adelaide. She thought I might like to go, and she offered to take on some of my classes so I could attend. Permission was granted, and another Abbotsleigh teacher and I travelled together by train. From 9 - 15 May, we took part in Adelaide University's 'New Perspectives in Music Education'.

One of the speakers and workshop leaders was British composer, performer and music educator Richard Orton—my soulmate.

CHAPTER 7

A NEW RELATIONSHIP AND A NEW COUNTRY

Richard gave an address on the first day of the conference. He was a lecturer at York University in England, where he'd founded an electronic music studio. He spoke well and had the most beautiful speaking voice. I'd enrolled for a workshop he ran, and I played the cello in it when the group performed 'new music' with nontraditional notation. Our session ended late afternoon, and those of us who were visitors to Adelaide decided to have a meal together. We all went to a nearby pizza restaurant. When we placed our orders at the counter it turned out that Richard, like me, was a vegetarian—the only ones in the group. We got talking. I felt as if I'd known him all my life. Richard invited me to join him the following night at a formal dinner being given for the speakers and workshop leaders. So, at the end of the conference, I sat beside him at that dinner and we talked much more.

A NEW RELATIONSHIP AND A NEW COUNTRY

Richard was to visit university music departments in Sydney, as well as other capital cities, before returning to England.

'We must meet up when you're in Sydney', I said. 'We'll take you for a drive to the Blue Mountains'. I gave him our home phone number and made a note of the dates he expected to be there. And when Richard arrived, we did take him for a drive to see Katoomba's Three Sisters, the Wentworth Falls and other beautiful places in the mountains west of Sydney. And we invited him to join us for a meal at my sister's place in Cremorne, where he met Tina, her husband, their children and my mother. He fitted in well.

Richard was married and had two young children, similar in ages to Martin and Wendy. He missed them and enjoyed being with our children. Wendy was particularly drawn to him, holding his hand much of the time.

I went to an evening concert at Sydney University, which Richard had been invited to. I sat beside him in the audience, with Peter Sculthorpe's mother on the other side. After the concert, Richard gave his apologies to Peter and, instead of attending the reception, he and I walked through the city, stopping for a hot chocolate at a cafe, and ending up at his hotel in King's Cross.

We talked and talked. Words can't describe the connection we felt with one another. We knew the other's thoughts, could feel the other's feelings, and the physical attraction was now incredibly strong. But we were both married to other people, and neither of us had ever considered being unfaithful. In those days virginity before marriage was the norm, and we'd only ever had one partner. I was not willing, that night, to be unfaithful to Tony, or to cause Richard to be unfaithful to his wife.

I got home from the city at three in the morning, and I remember the strange mixture of thoughts and emotions as I taught school classes that morning. I'd only had a couple hours of sleep, but there was plenty of adrenaline driving me. I was on a high.

Richard moved on to Melbourne, where he was to have a free weekend. He phoned and asked me to fly down and stay with him at his city hotel. I told Tony, and he actually encouraged me to say yes! He even drove me to the airport to get my plane. Tony told me later,

'I knew you had a close spiritual connection with Richard, but I expected a physical relationship would not work out.'

That weekend was unreal. The plane was delayed two hours, and Tony and I met a number of our friends while waiting at the airport. In Melbourne, along with lots of conversation, Richard and I did make love—and it was wonderful. I felt complete. I wanted to be with him for the rest of my life, and he felt the same way about me.

Of course, Tony was devastated when he was driving me home from the airport on the Sunday evening and learned how things had developed. At one point he pulled the car over to the kerb, and got out to vent his feelings and calm down before continuing.

A NEW RELATIONSHIP AND A NEW COUNTRY

Richard and I wrote letters to one another during the rest of his time in Australia. The night he arrived back in England, he told his wife that he was very tired, and he went off to bed alone. He'd been away for some weeks, and she was highly suspicious. Once the children had gone to bed she went through his bags and found the letters I'd written. She immediately woke Richard and confronted him. He admitted he'd been unfaithful and wanted to be with me.

They discussed the situation. Tony and I discussed the situation. Letters were written—but, of course, it was usually three weeks between posting and receiving the replies. Richard had had 'writer's block' with his composing. He and his wife both believed that my being with him would put an end to that. She actually wrote to me and suggested I move to England. Richard's choice was for us all to play 'happy families', with him still with his wife and children, but with me and mine in the same house. This idea did not appeal to me or to his wife. Eventually it was decided I would go to York and would live in a rented house belonging to friends of his, close to the university. The owners were living and working with Krishnamurti in the south of England, and would only be returning occasionally, at which time the children and I would go on holiday.

I was very much 'in my head' at this time. I desperately wanted to do what was best for everyone, rather than just follow my desires. I used a pendulum or I Ching sticks to make the major decisions.

JUST AN ORDINARY PERSON

It was agreed that Martin and Wendy would stay with me. However, Gordon, then fourteen, was a ward of the state, and needed his mother's permission to leave the country. When she was told I was moving to England, she asked for Gordon to be returned to her and his biological father, who was again living with her.

'No way will I allow him to go overseas', she said. I was glad that we'd prepared him from the beginning for the possible return to her.

In December 1971, Tony bravely and cheerfully took us to Circular Quay's overseas passenger terminal, and waved as we threw streamers from the deck as our ship left Sydney for Southampton via the Panama Canal. After a couple of days of seasickness, Martin, Wendy and I enjoyed our four-week voyage. I joined the Greek dancing and yoga classes, and played the piano accompaniment for a flute player at an onboard concert. There were many activities for the children, too. Apart from problems with the ship's air-conditioning, it was a perfect holiday for us all. I made some friends—one of whom joined us for the days ashore in Auckland and New York, and later visited us in England.

Many of the passengers were English migrants returning to their homeland. They'd come over, as had Tony and his parents twenty-three years earlier, as '£10 poms'. At that time, Australia had a 'White Australia' policy due to a fear that Asians would overtake the country if allowed to permanently live here. So, in order to help populate Australia, our government and the British government had devised a scheme by which over a million UK migrants

A NEW RELATIONSHIP AND A NEW COUNTRY

would travel here between 1945 and 1972. They came by ship and by plane, the total cost being just £10 per person—to cover processing fees. Future Australian prime ministers Gillard and Abbott arrived this way, as well as businessman Alan Bond and actor Hugh Jackman's parents.

But many migrants were disappointed once they were here. They'd expected Australia to be like England but with more sunshine and higher temperatures. It wasn't. And they weren't generally well received by the locals. A number of the so-called 'whinging Poms' were on our ship heading back to their homeland, families and friends. Martin and Wendy met up with some children who were returning to Yorkshire and, by the time we reached England, my two Aussie children had strong Yorkshire accents.

Our new home was not far from where Richard and his family lived. At first, he stayed with them but spent a lot of time with us—and sometimes overnight. But after a few weeks he moved in permanently, though his discomfort and guilt at being with me meant that he wouldn't answer the phone or the door. And when we were in public together and Richard saw someone he knew, he would leave me. It even happened in London, more than 200 miles from home. We'd gone down for a concert and, afterwards, when he saw a friend, he just walked away from me and I had to get a train back by myself. Richard actually threatened to kill me if I spoke to anyone he knew. He was clearly tortured. And I was becoming more and more of a 'doormat', my self-esteem and confidence reducing by the day. I'd become one of those wives who was fearful of displeasing her husband. I would spend hours finely chopping carrots and other vegetables into matchsticks for the macrobiotic meals he preferred, and I made sure his food was ready to dish up the moment he walked in the door. I'd be anxiously looking through the window watching for his arrival.

* * *

I received news from Australia that the outcome for Gordon was not good. His parents had had another child, a boy, since losing the older three to foster homes. This youngest child didn't take kindly to suddenly having an older brother around. According to Gordon, the young boy did a lot of naughty things and told his parents that Gordon had done them. Instead of enjoying a loving welcome, Gordon was constantly being criticised, punished and excluded. And they got him to visit a number of our friends in an effort to get financial help from them. Gordon had to say that he would be taken from his mother if she didn't have more money. Some of the friends told Tony what was happening. The child welfare department investigated, and it was decided that Gordon's biological parents were not fit to have custody of him.

Tony was not permitted to have Gordon live with him as he was 'single' and working full-time; there was no pre-school or after-school care in those days. So Gordon was placed in a boarding school for state wards. Later, when Tony remarried and moved to Victoria, where his parents still lived, he legally adopted Gordon, who then was able to live with him and finish his schooling in Victoria. Interestingly, Tony's wife was Marianne, the friend who'd

A NEW RELATIONSHIP AND A NEW COUNTRY

been responsible for my meeting Richard, and who'd sung with us at our Wahroonga house.

Even though Tony and I had failed to produce children in our fourteen years of marriage, he and Marianne clearly had no difficulty conceiving. Gordon enjoyed being big brother to their three young children, though after he left school he joined a circus and left home. We've not seen or officially heard from him since. There were rumours that he had been involved in a scam at the time of the Newcastle earthquake. And there were rumours of his being seriously ill. None of the family knows of his present whereabouts or circumstances.

* * *

Martin, Wendy and I had been in York for about six months when my mother came to visit and take the children and me on a trip through the Loire Valley in France. We took my car across the channel and stayed in Amsterdam and Paris before visiting all those lovely chateaux.

Before we left home my mother talked seriously to me about my difficult relationship with Richard, and she convinced me to leave him and move back to Australia. I even wrote to enquire about returning to my former teaching job. But once we'd got back to London, where Richard met us, my longing to be with him caused me to change my mind again. I told myself (and my mother) that the good times made up for the bad ones. And so we continued, Richard and I both full of guilt over breaking our wedding vows and hurting our spouses and our children. My guilt was probably worse, because I wasn't even aware of it at the time. I had regrets, but no realisation of anything deeper.

***

Not long after my mother's return to Australia, I became pregnant. This was nothing like the scenes I'd seen at the movies all my life—with congratulations, cigars handed out, booties being knitted, happy smiles all round. I was not married. Richard was so devastated by the ending of his first marriage that he'd decided never to marry again. He certainly didn't want the responsibility of more children. I had been wanting all my life to give birth to a baby, and was faced with a huge dilemma.

Richard's wife was very supportive. She and I actually got on very well together. She told me that I must keep the baby. Richard wanted me to have an abortion while he was away on a pre-arranged holiday with her and their children. He also told me he wasn't sure if he'd be coming back to us. To make matters worse, my mother in Australia wrote and told me I must not bring a baby into the world if it wasn't wanted by both parents. In her beautifully typed, blue onion-skin airmail letter she gave me the address of the place in London where I must go for an abortion. That's when I learned that she'd had an abortion after conceiving again when Tina was just four months old. Abortion was illegal in Australia then, but my mother didn't believe they could provide financially for a third child. For thirty-six years she had told no one.

A NEW RELATIONSHIP AND A NEW COUNTRY

I was shocked and confused! But I wasn't able to take my mother's advice, distressed as I was. I allowed the pregnancy to continue. My landlord had given notice that he was returning permanently to the house I was renting in York. Before moving out, I went to the library and got information on de facto relationships, and with Martin and Wendy I settled into our second rental property—a large country farmhouse north of York—using Richard's surname and telling my new neighbours that my husband was away. Fortunately, he did return to us.

But this was no 'white picket fence' and happily-ever-after scenario. Our happy times were few and far between. Our family was dysfunctional at times as we struggled in our love-hate relationship.

Having been a vegetarian and follower of natural health principles for some ten years, I visited a recommended naturopath during my pregnancy. He was not permitted to deliver babies, but told me of an amazing place where I could go to give birth naturally. And so I met Olive—a woman who was to play a most important role in my life, and in the life of my biological children.

Nurse Olive Rodgers was seventy-four years old when I first met her. She looked like a very stern school ma'am, her hair tied back in a small bun and her 'no-nonsense' attitude apparent from the start. I was thirty-seven, but felt like a child of seven as I faced her after my 200-mile drive from York to Buckinghamshire. Olive had previously worked in London with two highly esteemed naturopathic doctors. After their deaths she had been in such demand for home births that a group of mothers had got together, bought a farm, and set her up in this farmhouse where up to three women could have 'home births' at any one time. There was room for the fathers to stay if they wished to attend the birth, and a large nursery where any young siblings could be accommodated for the full two or three weeks. No baby left Olive's until it was sleeping through the night and successfully breastfeeding.

I handed Olive the medical form on which the York doctor had described me as 'an elderly primate', and sat down for my interview. I answered all her questions honestly. She learned of my lifelong longing to have a baby, my failure to conceive in my first marriage, my move to England after falling in love with the baby's father, his views, my mother's views. All of it. Olive showed no reaction, but my application was accepted, and I drove back to Yorkshire with a list of everything I had to make or buy for the baby. I was given precise details of numbers and brands of cotton nappies, gauze nappies, cotton nighties, and pure wool knitted items that I was to bring when I next came—for the rehearsal! The chaff-filled mattress she would organise for me.

I'd first read all available books about having a baby naturally some seventeen years earlier, but now I was studying it in earnest. I attended local classes where we not only learned of the various stages of labour and how best to breath at each stage, but also had lots of practice in relaxing and breathing a certain way while the pain of labour was simulated through Chinese burns. So when the time came for my next visit to Olive, I was somewhat more confident, and she was quite satisfied with my performance.

A NEW RELATIONSHIP AND A NEW COUNTRY

As my due date approached, my mother came from Australia to look after the older children. Three days after the baby was due, and following a slight 'show', Richard and I shared the long drive to Olive's farm. Richard wanted to be at the birth. I felt awful about the fact that he had a first performance of a musical composition that night, and my mother had just had her hair done with a view to accompanying him and hearing his music for the first time. But, clearly, it was my 'first performance' that had to take priority.

After arrival at Olive's and a brief external examination, she said it could be days before the baby's arrival. She suggested that Richard stay overnight at a local hotel, and that I sleep on the delivery table she had set up for me. Another family was there, and no beds were ready. We went to a nearby restaurant, phoned my mother, discussed returning home next morning, ate an enormous meal, and Richard dropped me off at the farmhouse at 10 pm.

The delivery table was narrow and hard, and I was most uncomfortable. I began to regret having eaten so much. But it wasn't long before it dawned on me that my discomfort was actually labour. I began my special breathing, mentally counting backwards; then about an hour later I pressed the bedside buzzer and summoned Olive.

It was a short labour. Calm, quiet and completely without interference. There was no shaving, no enemas, no internal examinations with Olive, and she didn't cut umbilical cords until they'd stopped pulsing and the afterbirth had come away naturally. I remember being in a state of total disbelief as I exclaimed, 'I can't believe I'm having a baby!' as my healthy nine-pounder emerged.

My firstborn came into the world at 5:15 a.m. on 22 March 1973. He was wrapped and placed in a crib in the corner of the room, where he slept soundly for over twelve hours. Richard arrived soon after 8 am and waited all day for the baby to wake. He actually did some gentle prodding from time to time. When the little one woke at 6:30 pm, Richard held him, looked at him and named him Simon.

Olive usually did all the laundry and cleaning at West Farm, having help only when the farmhouse was full. But she alone cooked all the delicious and wholesome meals, and looked after the mothers, the new babies and any other children. In my eyes she was a wonder woman. We mothers spent most of our time in bed, so it was Olive who brought the babies into our room when she wanted them fed, who burped them until we became expert, who weighed them before and after each feed, and who bathed them until the second-last day, when we did it under her supervision. Much of my time in bed was spent copying out her mouthwatering recipes—the Leek and Cheese Pie, the Apple Pancakes, the dessert omelette served with a blob of homemade jam. I was very happy with every aspect of my 'confinement' at West Farm. And before I left there, Richard asked me to marry him. I was extremely pleased about that and, of course, I said yes. But I was most disappointed that he insisted the wedding be after the registration of the baby's birth, and not before it.

A NEW RELATIONSHIP AND A NEW COUNTRY

His wife had already remarried. She'd met someone while Richard was in Australia meeting me. They'd been very drawn to one another, but she hadn't let anything develop at the time. Once she learned of Richard's unfaithfulness, she'd allowed the new relationship to grow, and six weeks after I became pregnant to Richard, she conceived her third child. Both divorces had gone through, and she'd remarried before her baby was born. She'd always wanted more children, but Richard had been adamant they stop at two. With her new husband she had another three—two girls and a boy.

***

I returned to midwife Olive's the following year for the birth of my second child. Because of the quick first labour, I drove down with twenty-one-month-old Simon a few days before the due date. I took my sewing machine and did some sewing, and I spent a lot of time with Simon playing with 'Teach Your Baby to Read' and 'Teach Your Baby Maths' flash cards. Every day Olive drove the two of us, and a pram, a couple miles away from the farmhouse and dropped us off. I had to walk back with Simon in the pram to ensure I got my daily exercise and fresh air. It was wintertime. This went on for over two weeks. My mother had arrived in York. Richard was impatient. But no way was Olive going to induce a birth.

'If you want the baby to come before it's ready, you'll have to go elsewhere', she said.

There was another family staying at West Farm at that time. I'd been socialising with them and was invited to join them on a day out to a safari park. Olive gave her permission, and I spent the whole day sitting in the front seat of their Land Rover with Simon on my lap, no exercise whatever. I felt a bit uncomfortable after dinner that night, but watched a film made by the other couple—he was a director and she an actress. As I prepared for bed, my 'waters broke'. It was about 11 pm. Olive phoned Richard so he could drive down for the birth, and she set me up on the delivery table, got the basinet ready, then went back to bed. Richard woke her when he arrived; she brought him up to the delivery room then went downstairs to make him a cup of tea. But the tea was never made. This time Richard pressed the buzzer for me, and Olive returned just in time to deliver another healthy boy (at 5:05 am on 8 December, 1974).

This baby wasn't sleepy like the first one. He was wide awake and alert, and looked into Richard's eyes as his father held him until the cord was cut. My first baby was blue-eyed and fair. This one had deep brown eyes and dark brown hair. Richard named him Graeme.

It had been arranged for some time that we would all go to Aviemore in Scotland for Christmas and the New Year with my mother and my sister's oldest son, who had flown to England with her. My mother was gifting us all this holiday. Graeme's later-than-expected arrival meant leaving Buckinghamshire a little earlier than Olive would have liked. But the baby was feeding well and sleeping through the nights, and we agreed to travel by car while the rest of the family took the train there and back.

CHAPTER 8

A MOVE, AN AFFAIR, AND A '*HANDICAPPED*' CHILD

*T*here were many stressful events and some very traumatic ones during the three-plus years before our next baby was born. First of all, we moved house. Richard and I were at a concert at the university and, at interval, learned that an artist friend of his was selling his property on the other side of York. Richard had been there and loved the place. After phoning the owner, we skipped the second half of the concert and drove there for an inspection—and we immediately made arrangements to buy the property. The house had originally been the Wheelwright's Cottage. A spacious and sunny room with arched chapel windows had been added at the back where the barn had been. There was the apprentice's room, accessible by a fold-up ladder. The grounds were vast, with a very large orchard, impressive vegetable gardens, a running 'stream' for growing watercress, a fish pond and, on one side of the house, a gorgeous green lawn the size of a normal block of land. We later learned that the chapel whose windows were incorporated into the back room of the house, had been originally located on that side block. In the outbuildings behind the house, there was room for a car, Wendy's horse and our goat—and a rack for a boat. (There was a river nearby.) To top it off, a lovely old gardener came with the property; he worked for free in return for being able to take fruit and veggies home for himself and his adult daughter.

But life was far from idyllic for me. Immediately after the move, Richard insisted I paint the inside walls, cut up and freeze the surplus apples, and make jam from the ripe raspberries and blackberries. On top of looking after the four children, one of whom was still crawling, it all became too much. I decided to engage a local woman to help me with the ironing. But the day before she was to come, I picked up a large pile of dinner plates and smashed them onto the floor. I then threw myself down and cried. Richard called the doctor and an appointment was made for me for two weeks later! The doctor prescribed medication, and the nurse/receptionist told me I should be grateful for all that I had—not complaining.

I took the tablets but, having not had so much as one aspirin in thirteen years, this 'mind-altering' and 'calming down' medication just knocked me out. I couldn't get out of bed. A neighbour contacted the doctor and the tablets were changed, but I still had no energy at all. And yet, I was wanting to do the things I needed to do. On Christmas Day I couldn't serve any meals to the family, and I felt so guilty and out of control. The following day Richard's first

A MOVE, AN AFFAIR, AND A 'HANDICAPPED' CHILD

wife and her two young children visited us. I went through the motions of a hostess, feeling like a zombie. The following morning, standing at the bathroom basin, I slit my left wrist with a razor blade. There was a lot of blood but, incredibly, as I progressed with the cut I could see the wound closing up. I wasn't even able to end my life. (But talk about psychic surgery!)

Richard never ever acknowledged this incident, and he ignored me at the time. I desperately needed help so I phoned the naturopath, and he allowed me to stay at his premises for a couple of weeks. While there I rested a lot and was gradually weaned off the medication. Once back home, my local doctor insisted I see a psychiatrist, so I began regular visits as he endeavoured to find the cause of my difficulties.

* * *

When Graeme was just two, I had a miscarriage at home. Twin foetuses were clearly recognisable. I had to spend two nights in hospital as the doctor checked me out. I think it was shortly after that, that Richard began an affair. I have no desire or need to rake up old hurts. I now believe that everything we experience in life is, in a way, for our benefit; and is, in a way, of our own doing. But I'm mentioning this incident, as it gives an indication of the complexities of our relationship.

From the beginning of our marriage there'd been a thought in the back of my mind that, since I'd had an affair with him before we married, I must be prepared to accept any unfaithfulness from him in the future. Karma, and all that. There had even been times during our intimate conversations when I assured Richard that I would always love him unconditionally—no matter what. And so it was that one day he literally challenged me to be true to my word. Wow! I bottled up my emotions and was loving, caring and sympathetic after he told me, one calm and happy morning in bed, that he'd had a brief affair with a student when away teaching at an Open University. He assured me he was no longer in contact with her. It was all over.

Some months later, I learned the true facts. The affair was with his secretary, and was ongoing. And he'd even invited her home to lunch with us at the time I was on medication and so upset. He later said he'd hoped her 'counselling me' would help.

For many years, my goal and efforts to love unconditionally actually resulted in loads of resentment. My anger exploded at times, but I was holding down many strong emotions—guilt, shame and lack of self-worth, along with that resentment and anger. Mentally, I was in agony most days. My visits to the psychiatrist didn't seem to help. I was pleased to know I could offload my complaints at each visit, but usually, by the time the appointment came around, the offloading process was disappointing. Ironically, my married psychiatrist was having an affair with someone in our village. She became pregnant and gave birth. He divorced his wife. And he committed suicide.

A MOVE, AN AFFAIR, AND A 'HANDICAPPED' CHILD

I had another miscarriage (a very early one) the day after I arrived by myself in London for the 1977 Mind, Body & Spirit Festival. At this event, along with many interesting 'New Age' speakers, there was a group of people offering free 'spiritual healing'. I decided to join the queue for it, but was perplexed when they asked what I wanted healing for. I was in excellent physical health and found myself saying 'miscarriages'. And so the group silently surrounded me, positioning their hands a few inches away from my abdominal and pelvic area.

Not long after this, I conceived again. By now, Richard was thinking it would be nice if we had a daughter, and we'd looked at a kind of calendar that indicated the best days for conceiving a girl. The moment I told him I suspected I was pregnant, he said, 'It will be a Mongol' (at that time this was not a derogatory term, but the word used for people with Down syndrome). I was shocked. Obviously I was not happy at such a reception, but I actually thought no more of it. The weeks before the baby's due date I had a number of 'false labours'. A lot of pain, but not a true labour.

I don't recall just when I made my third and final trip to Olive's. But this time I took both Simon and Graeme with me, we got there in good time, and it was another quick and straightforward birth. My baby daughter was born at 11:50 pm on 18 February 1978. Richard had decided not to attend this time. And for the first time, he said that I could choose the baby's name. One of the many things I'd resented through the years was not being able to discuss names with him. He'd previously refused to talk about possible names, insisting that he make the decision once the babies were born. I didn't dare challenge him.

I had the greatest difficulty choosing a name that felt right. I had with me a book of children's names, and Olive lent me lists of names of flowers. For days I read through them all, becoming more and more frustrated. Nothing seemed to fit. As I write this I realise that that must have been my parents' dilemma—matching a name to a particular child. My baby girl seemed somehow different, special. Nothing seemed appropriate. Eventually I settled on Jennifer Elizabeth. We'd nearly called our adopted daughter 'Jennifer'. It was a name I'd always liked, and an 'Elizabeth' had watched this baby being born. She'd previously had difficult childbirths, and was at West Farm for a better experience. Olive wanted her to see how easy and straightforward childbirth can be, so towards the end of my labour, everything was put on hold (Olive told me to pant) while she ran off and got Elizabeth.

Law required that people giving birth at Olive's visit a local doctor some time before their due date. That doctor then went to West Farm a few days after the births to examine the babies and sign a certificate. The doctor I'd seen duly came and checked out Jennifer. The boys were in the room, and he commented that she had the family nose. Olive and I were aware that this baby was more floppy than the boys had been, and she didn't feed so easily. Olive actually asked me about the medication I'd had before I'd conceived.

A MOVE, AN AFFAIR, AND A 'HANDICAPPED' CHILD

I'd been back home for a couple of weeks when the district nurse came to see Jennifer and me. The next day I had a phone call from the doctor.

'We like to see the babies, you know.' An appointment was made for me to go with the baby to the surgery. The doctor examined Jennifer and was perplexed. He suspected a 'chromosomal disorder'. Her heart was strong but there were some indications of Down syndrome. He arranged for tests to be run. A problem with the first test meant a second one was needed. It took time for the culture to grow. And so it was six weeks before the results came through. Jennifer had high-grade Down syndrome.

The way it all happened was a blessing to me. From the beginning we'd bonded with our sweet little bundle of love, having no notion she would never be the 'normal' daughter we expected. And during those six weeks of uncertainty I'd read everything I could about this 'chromosomal disorder'. I'd read of parents who'd rejected their babies at birth—placing them in institutions, and of mothers who had killed their babies. But I also read books written by people with Down syndrome. My sister, back in Australia, was teaching disabled children at the time, and was most helpful. She sent over piles of information about early intervention programs. In York, just ten miles from us, the hospital offered weekly physiotherapy, and many other forms of assistance. They accepted us from day one. I also joined the local Down syndrome support group, where each week the babies were looked after while the mothers met and talked and shared experiences and information. So I was well supported. And the family all adored our latest addition.

JUST AN ORDINARY PERSON

However, the months following Jennifer's diagnosis were demanding for me. Every day I did the massaging of her arms and legs with warm oil, and exercised her limbs as I'd been instructed. Most nights I was hanging up the nappies on an indoor clothesline close to midnight before getting to bed. With hindsight, I realise it wouldn't have been the end of the world if I'd stopped baking the bread every day, stopped making and baking the muesli, prepared more simple meals. But I was being what I thought I should be.

Jennifer never cried. Not once do I recall her waking from a sleep and crying to be fed. (Graeme, when a baby, had cried loudly every time his nappy was wet.) And Jennifer gave us so much love. I can honestly say that the best experience in my whole life was when holding her close to my heart. I had a baby carrier that positioned her in front of me, facing in. Jennifer would spend most of her waking time there, contentedly, as I did my housework. And she clearly loved it when I sat at the piano and played and sang to her. It was only when she was tired that Jennifer had the Down syndrome facial appearance. I was surprised, though, on one of my visits to the hospital with her, when a stranger in the lift remarked, 'I wish I had one like that!'

This baby brought the family together; somehow, she drew the best out of everyone. Richard once said that she was the only one of his children he didn't feel threatened by. He felt a sense of inadequacy with the others. He'd regarded it his duty in his first marriage to have a son and a daughter. Richard once told me that when he was very young, he'd seen a most beautiful fish in a river and had taken it home to show his parents. Of course, it was dead by the

A MOVE, AN AFFAIR, AND A 'HANDICAPPED' CHILD

time he got there. He told himself, then and there, that he wasn't fit to be responsible for the life of another.

Jennifer's life was a short one. Unknown to us, a cold had quickly turned to bronchitis and pneumonia. Her death was quite unexpected. She was eleven-and-a-half months old. On the day she died we'd all taken her to York in Martin's new secondhand car, and she'd been fitted for spectacles. It was snowing that day, but Jennifer was warmly wrapped and in her carry cot on the floor of the car. I was a bit concerned at the fumes that seemed to be coming up from underneath, but she showed no signs of distress.

That evening, however, she didn't want to eat or drink anything, and she'd had very little all day. I remember sitting by the fireplace at 7 pm, Jennifer in her pram beside me, Richard working at his desk nearby. I was incredibly tired, but I was waiting to try her again with a bottle before putting her to bed for the night. Richard generously said, 'Go to bed, Dee. I'll give Jennifer her bottle before I come up later'. I prepared her cot with a hot water bottle (to be removed when she went in) and went to bed and into the deepest sleep. At about 11 pm I was woken by Richard gently touching my shoulder. Calmly and lovingly he said, 'Jennifer is dead. When I went to pick her up she was cold and stiff.' As he said the first three words, I was actually flooded with a feeling of peace and a kind of relief. But there was also the adrenaline that came when the extraordinary news registered. I got up and we talked about what steps we needed to take. I don't recall any details of the hours that followed, but I do recall that Richard was at his best, and fully supportive. We called the authorities. We were told nothing could be done until morning.

It was strange having a dead body in the house overnight. We took her upstairs and placed her on the single bed in her room. Jennifer looked as if she were sleeping, lying on her side, her back facing us. Next morning the other four children came and had a look at her. Once the authorities were involved, we were told that an autopsy would be required due to her sudden death and the fact that she'd not recently seen a doctor.

Richard was due to be away from home for a few days. It was another Open University commitment. I assured him I could handle everything, and encouraged him to go as planned—I functioned much better when he was not around. And I did cope extremely well. I made all the arrangements, shopped, thoroughly cleaned the house, was gracious to visitors and those who phoned, and with the older children I 'baked up a storm' in case people came back to our house after the funeral. But I did not like it when a friend from the next village sent me a 'happy' card and said, 'What a good thing to have happened!' It's true that at one level I was relieved that my load was lessened, and I was philosophical about death, in general—but I would have given anything to have had her back with me, just as she was. I was weeping a little one morning a few days afterwards, when Martin saw me. He'd adored Jennifer—he loved to just gaze at her. He said, 'Mum, you're a hypocrite. You know you wanted her dead'. It was the first time I'd heard Martin say

A MOVE, AN AFFAIR, AND A 'HANDICAPPED' CHILD

anything that wasn't complimentary. He'd always been my 'support person'. I understood how he felt. But I wasn't acting. I was grieving. As was he.

At 10 o'clock that morning an occupational therapist arrived for her first home visit to work with Jennifer. I'd phoned the hospital a couple days previously and told them of her death, but the message hadn't been passed on. The young woman was so upset. I ended up 'counselling' and supporting her, as Simon and Graeme played with the toys she'd brought for the baby.

The following day the funeral director phoned me and said, 'Jennifer is ready to be seen'. I was so surprised! He was expecting a viewing at the funeral parlour. He told me that he and his staff had spent a lot of time preparing her to be seen. I realised I'd better go. Someone should see her. But I was not prepared for what I saw.

In a beautiful little coffin, lined with frilly lace, my baby daughter had been 'made up'. Lipstick, rouge and a hairstyle she'd never had! I realised they'd gone to a lot of trouble, but this was, to me, grotesque. I thanked them. But I was so glad the coffin was to be closed at the funeral and that others would remember her as she'd been.

Richard returned home, and the following day we woke to blue skies and sunshine, though the ground was covered in ice. Jennifer's funeral service was attended by many of our friends and neighbours. St Michael's was the only church in the village, and it was very much a community meeting place; there, people shared their news, joys and sorrows. No one came back to the house afterwards. We were surprised and at first disappointed, but later were very pleased, as the six of us spent time together in our clean and inviting house—and with all that food.

CHAPTER 9

FUN AND GAMES AS CHILDREN PLAY

Very soon after Jennifer's death, my life changed again. We were at home alone one day when Richard made an announcement. 'Dee, now that you don't have Jennifer to look after, it's time you started earning some money. You can give piano lessons from home.'

'Oh, no', I thought. But I said nothing. I felt sick to the stomach. So disappointed.

I knew we were struggling a bit with finances, paying back the money my parents had lent us to buy our beautiful house, and Richard was paying maintenance money to his other two children. But I'd hoped for some spare time at last. Some time alone. For so many years, I'd been woken up by someone needing my attention. I used to long to be able to sit and relax and have a cuppa when I returned from shopping, but the moment I walked in the door, someone would be making demands.

I didn't want to teach piano for many reasons. I hadn't trained as a piano teacher, though I'd specialised in music at university and had taught music as a subject in schools. I felt unqualified and inadequate. I'd been an untrained school teacher, and now was looking at being an untrained piano teacher. But I wouldn't have dreamed of refusing and displeasing Richard. I needed his approval. Richard needed to be in control; at times he even took our little television set to work with him to ensure I didn't watch it when he wasn't at home. I thought that was ironic—watching TV is the last thing I would have been doing. I had so much on my plate.

I reluctantly agreed. Richard himself was a qualified piano teacher, but had never taught. His interest was in working with adults, not children. His university lecturing suited him to the ground. He obviously thought I was capable.

I prepared myself by attending a school holiday residential course for piano teachers. There, I became familiar with the English music exam system and its requirements, and learned a lot about the repertoire and how to teach it. And it was such a fun week, especially at the end when we participants put on a concert just for ourselves. Anyone could put their name down to perform. We had a trumpeter who was so nervous he couldn't control his mouth, and not one note came out of his instrument as he 'played' his piece to a piano accompaniment. And there was a very old lady pianist who never stopped. Every time we thought she'd come to the end of her

FUN AND GAMES AS CHILDREN PLAY

tedious piece, she turned another page and carried on! The audience was in hysterics, but trying to hide it.

We lived in an isolated village, and there was no shortage of children wanting piano lessons. In fact, by the time I left England nine years later (my mind firmly made up never again to teach piano), I had forty-five pupils a week. By then we'd moved to a new house further down the street. I was paying a girl to come and mind the children after school, as Martin and Wendy were no longer at home. I paid for house cleaning twice a week, and I paid a gardener to mow and weed.

I actually enjoyed those years of teaching, and did it well. My pupils seemed to enjoy it, too, and those who chose to do exams got very high marks. I liked the one-to-one time with them. Along with teaching most of the local children, I also gave lessons to some of the parents, including the new local vicar.

But there was always some resentment at the back of my mind. I was trying to be unconditionally loving all the time. I wasn't in touch with my feelings, and was very much in my head, constantly judging myself and finding fault. I remember noticing my reflection in shop windows whenever I was shopping in York. I always looked so unhappy. Mouth down at the corners, face tense, eyes so dull. I didn't like what I saw, but I couldn't make my face change. I'd look at the people around me with their happy faces, and feel even more miserable. I believed any degree of physical pain would be preferable to my almost unbearable emotional pain and mental anguish.

JUST AN ORDINARY PERSON

When I was with my pupils, I snapped out of it, of course. But most days when I awoke, I truly wished and prayed that I were dead.

*　*　*

Soon after the piano lessons started, my voluntary 'youth work' began. Gosh! Again I was untrained, though, as the years went on, I undertook a number of courses in various aspects of youth work. And, in fact, I had a natural aptitude for it.

Some local teenagers had announced publicly that they wanted a meeting place where they could play table tennis, listen to music and generally socialise. Our tiny village had only one general store in the front of a private house, along with one church and two pubs. Later on, a post office operated from the front room of another private house. But that was it. There was nowhere indoors where young people could gather. There was no public transport other than a Monday-to-Friday bus for city workers—one bus to York early morning, and one bus back in the evening. Even though we were only a fifteen-minute drive from the city of York, we were 'isolated'. An official meeting was held in the village hall, and it was decided that the young ones could only meet in that hall if supervised by an adult. These were some of the 'most difficult' of the local kids. No adult put their hand up to spend a night a week with them.

The local minister and his wife invited them to meet as a Youth Club at the rectory, and they obtained some table tennis tables and a record player. But a couple of evenings there was enough for these young people. They were 'Bible bashed' for a good hour before any games or socialising took place. The rector's hopes to convert them were dashed. In fact, very soon afterwards the church was vandalised and from then on the door was locked.

I was the secretary of the Village Hall Association. I heard what had happened, and I offered to go to the hall each Saturday night and be there while the youth group met. 'Everyone' wanted to join—the prospective members were aged four to twenty-four. So I formed three groups: the youngest ones came first in the early evening; and the young adults came last. In time, the older ones got mopeds and went further afield, and I ran just two groups.

From the beginning, my young sons, Simon and Graeme, were members. For nine years my Saturday nights were spent at the hall enjoying my role of voluntary youth worker. For most of those years the new vicar came and assisted when he was free; he was a people person, an amateur actor, and was popular with everyone. He joined our management committee and was a great asset.

I loved the work. I enjoyed reading about the grants available, preparing grant applications, and arranging for visiting professionals to come and work with the children. I was happy planning each night's activities, setting up the hall and making it inviting, and arranging a roster of parents to assist me. And I loved the time spent with the children, facilitating, encouraging, soothing and having fun together. For twenty years my favourite book had been 'A Child and his Play'. It was full of ideas, and covered many topics. There were word games, memory games, cooking suggestions and recipes, and many physically active games. I was most happy when enabling children to play and have fun, and it was a great escape from my marital conflicts. I now realise that this demanding work brought me into 'the present' and left me no time for dwelling on past or future difficulties with Richard.

It wasn't long before my youth work included weekend or school holiday residential adventures. Once a year I would take our sheltered village children to a former priory in the Yorkshire Dales, where they would go potholing, abseiling and wall-climbing, and had lessons in archery and canoeing. They also learned a few domestic tasks as they made their beds, helped set tables and washed up. And everyone helped clean the premises before leaving. One boy hadn't known a sink had a plug to insert before use; two of the teenage girls had never used a broom before—they boarded at a private school. Being away from their parents, there were also opportunities to become more independent, to learn to accept minor mishaps and to observe the behaviour of other children twenty-four hours a day. I found it interesting watching the behaviour of one little girl. She was an only child—a very beautiful 'doll-like' girl with her pale face, pink cheeks and long blond curly hair. Her parents doted on her, and I'd previously seen how she would run to them at the slightest difficulty. On the trip with us, on a walk to the potholes and miles away from her family, she scratched a finger. Well, the way she carried on! You'd have thought it was the end of the world. She cried and screamed 'Mummy' at the top of her voice. I was quite low-key as I comforted her and applied a plaster. During

FUN AND GAMES AS CHILDREN PLAY

the days that followed she saw other children have minor accidents and take them in their stride. What a difference one week made in the life of that little girl.

I had a video camera in the 1980s. It was a fairly large piece of equipment that sat on my shoulder. I would film all of the group's activities while we were away and, at the end of the stay, once all was cleaned, packed and ready to go, everyone would gather together and watch the recording. It was always a calm and perfect ending to our adventurous holiday.

Another popular place for our away trips had a much more structured program. Its main feature was an assault course (elevated planks, logs over rivers, ropes up trees). There were many trust and group 'games', and a number of challenges requiring lateral thinking, where small groups would compete. The facility did cater for children, but it was mainly business colleagues who undertook its recreational and team-building courses. I was close to fifty when I first made a booking for our Youth Club members. I had not been aware that groups couldn't attend until their leaders had previously experienced the program. So the next thing I knew, in the middle of an English winter, I was doing the assault course along with other leaders—and walking a narrow plank while tied to an enormous woman I'd never met before. This was scary. It wasn't just up to me to keep my balance. My partner slipped. We hit the cold, muddy ground together, my jaws closing tight as I landed. All of my teeth were slightly chipped (my dentist later smoothed off the rough edges). But I soldiered on. I climbed a wall, I abseiled, I let myself fall off a high wall into the arms of the people below. That was not easy for me. But worst of all, I was told to climb an extremely high ladder and 'go out on a limb' sliding on my bottom, then drop, while attached to a harness. I've always feared heights. I couldn't leave the top of that ladder and I sheepishly climbed back down.

The kids loved every aspect of their time there, of course, and I enjoyed watching them, supervising and filming their activities. On their last weekend they were able to go horse riding at a nearby stables. None of them had been on a horse before; our little farming village had lots of cows and pigs and chickens, but horses were a rarity.

We probably had two residential excursions a year for several years. But there were also many 'away' events involving other youth clubs. These included overnight orienteering (a favourite, and one for which there was a lot of instruction from one of the fathers), and competitions in first aid, fire safety and cooking. Two of our members went to London to compete in the finals of a national cooking competition, where they had to cook a dish of their own creation. And the whole group won a national award for the diversity and quality of its activities—I had submitted a video as our entry.

Being a musician, I was also able to put on a number of shows that our members performed for the public in the adjoining village, where there was a large hall with a stage. There were some wonderful scripted musicals written for children, and I usually chose ones on environmental subjects. In our first show, the performers were endangered animals. I had experts come and show how to make the papier mache heads and costumes. A drama coach worked with them on their movements and stage positions/blocking. We had professional advice and tuition in making the scenery and props. I taught the songs and organised the little 'orchestra' to play the accompaniment.

I'll forever be grateful to the County Council for the money made available at that time to support voluntary youth groups. Our local children benefited so much from the professional instruction in many indoor and outdoor sports and activities.

CHAPTER 10

UNEXPECTED AND UNWELCOME EVENTS

Martin and Wendy both had visits back to the family in Australia in their mid-teens. Martin's trip back in 1974 was not without incident. His plane was grounded for repairs in Hong Kong, and all the passengers were transferred to hotels. At just fourteen, Martin found himself sharing a room with a stranger who persuaded him to carry one of his parcels through customs on arrival in Sydney. Of course, the customs officer decided to open that particular parcel, and it contained cigarettes. Martin was under age to smoke in Australia, but fortunately things were soon sorted out.

Wendy's travel experiences, however, had serious consequences. During her 1979 visit to see the family in Australia, she conceived a child. None of us knew anything of her situation until she phoned me immediately after a positive diagnosis from a doctor

UNEXPECTED AND UNWELCOME EVENTS

in the city of York—when she was already five months pregnant. Wendy told me that she hadn't suspected it herself until then. And she definitely wanted an abortion.

At the time, Wendy had left school and was pursuing studies in art and design. I made an offer to look after the baby while she continued her course. It was only a few months after Jennifer's death and I still had all the baby paraphernalia (pram, cot, clothes) and was at home all day. Surprisingly to me, by law I had no say in the matter. Wendy had now turned sixteen, and we were told that the decision to terminate or not was entirely up to her. So an abortion was arranged. But by the time all the paperwork was done and an appointment made, it was too late.

So Wendy decided that after a natural birth her baby would be given up for adoption. A social worker sat with us in the kitchen one day and the forms were filled in. I listened as Wendy gave a description of the baby's father—his height, build and colouring. She said it was someone she met for the first time when in Sydney.

Wendy went to the childbirth preparation classes I'd attended, and I agreed to be her 'support person' for a hospital birth. One morning, very close to her due date, she had a big argument with Richard. I have no recollection of what it was about. Heated arguments involving Wendy, Richard or me were common occurrences, unfortunately. The young boys had already left for school; Richard, Wendy and I were in the kitchen. Richard was still sitting at the breakfast table when Wendy completely 'lost it' and hit him on the back of his head with a bottle of milk. (He ended up at the doctor's to have bits of glass extracted.) I went straight into maternal/protective mode.

'Wendy. Get your bag for the hospital and get into the car,' I told her. I grabbed my things, rushed out, and drove off with her to a neighbour's house, where I was expected for a morning meeting. Wendy was able to relax there quietly, and join us for some lunch, before I drove her to her prenatal appointment at the hospital.

The doctor there was concerned at her state and insisted she be admitted and induced. I spoke up.

'I'm happy for her to stay, Doctor. I think it's best for her and the baby. But I'm not in favour of the birth being induced'.

'You're happy for the baby to die, are you?' was his crushing response. Fortunately, labour began naturally before the induction team arrived. Once Wendy was settled in her bed, we just had time for a couple of games of Scrabble together before she was taken off to the delivery room.

Sadly, this birth was far from the natural one we'd expected. The room was brightly lit, it was noisy, there were people everywhere. Wendy was connected internally and externally to monitoring machines, and at her first painful contractions the nurse insisted she be given gas.

'No. She wants to have the baby naturally', I informed the nurse. I remembered the time when, giving birth to Simon, I would have said yes if offered pain relief. I was so glad it hadn't been an

UNEXPECTED AND UNWELCOME EVENTS

option—that I'd been helped to relax instead. I wanted to support Wendy in her choice.

'How can you want your daughter to be in pain when it's not necessary?' was the nurse's response. I felt crushed and helpless again.

Wendy fought and screamed as they tried to put the mask on her face, but eventually she went 'out to it'. The baby was delivered by forceps. He was weighed as I stood beside the scales and saw him for the first time. And I immediately realised who the father was. It wasn't the man described to the social worker. There can be such a strong resemblance in those first moments, before newborns just look like babies. This baby was the image of Gordon, her foster brother. Being jaundiced, the little boy was immediately taken off and given a blood transfusion, then placed in the intensive care unit, as it was empty at the time. The nurses made sure Wendy didn't see the baby, but her maternal instinct had kicked in. She insisted on caring for her son until she left the hospital. She changed him and gave him his bottles; she gave him love, until she was discharged.

Wendy confirmed my belief that Gordon was the father, so when I arrived home after the birth, I made a long-distance phone call to Australia and talked to Tony (my ex-husband and, legally, Wendy's father). He straight away spoke to Gordon, who was with him, and came back to the phone.

JUST AN ORDINARY PERSON

'Gordon says he's done some terrible things in his life, but he would never do that'. (Sexual relations between fostered/adopted children was illegal, even though there is no biological connection.)

'But if Wendy decides to keep the baby,' Tony continued, 'Gordon says he will contribute to its support'. In fact, Tony very much wanted her to keep the baby. He suggested she breastfeed him for a few months, then let the baby be looked after by his family in Victoria until Wendy was in a position to care for him herself. Wendy had no desire to accept this offer. She believed it was best for everyone for the adoption to proceed as planned.

Meanwhile, in our house, there was turmoil. Richard announced that Wendy was never to return home. I pleaded with him. I racked my brain to find a solution. Our local minister was away on leave, but I'd read in the newspaper of a very learned minister of religion who was a counsellor. I contacted him and an appointment was made for him to come to our house and speak to Richard the day before Wendy was due to leave hospital. Richard was furious, and said he wouldn't talk to the man.

I was so frustrated that one morning, as Richard walked out of the house when I implored him to talk about the situation, I tried to call out to him for help. And nothing came out of my mouth. I had lost my ability to speak. Never have I felt so helpless. For several days I walked around with pencil and paper in my pocket. I physically couldn't make a sound with my voice.

UNEXPECTED AND UNWELCOME EVENTS

This was the time when our two young sons, Simon and Graeme, bonded together. Aged five and seven, any former jealousy was left behind as they turned to each other for support. Their parents were no longer emotionally available to them. There was a funny side to it, though. The boys invited their friends around to see me! A mother who can't talk.

I continued to visit Wendy in hospital, and to act as if she would be returning home. And the day came for the counsellor's visit. Richard did meet him and was impressed. They talked privately. Richard agreed to have Wendy back. As he was leaving, the minister shook my hand and said, 'You can talk now'. And once he had gone, I could. My psychosomatic symptoms had gone.

Richard and Wendy had always had a love/hate relationship. When they first met in Australia they were inseparable. She was four. He was missing his young children and enjoyed being with mine—a boy and girl of similar age. Wendy was happy that we would be with Richard when we moved to England. But on arrival in Southampton, he hadn't been there to meet us. We'd been on the deck looking and waiting. Wendy was devastated. It was three hours after we docked that Richard appeared.

'The place I stayed at overnight didn't serve breakfast until eight', he explained. He clearly had cold feet.

Once we were all together, Richard began relating to Martin and Wendy as if they were his own. But one day he said that in the future he would not regard himself as any kind of a father to them.

JUST AN ORDINARY PERSON

And that's what he did, a lot of the time, though I do recall many happy evenings once we were married when everyone was gathered around the fireside, and Richard read Martin and Wendy *The Hobbit*, *The Lord of the Rings* and other similar classics.

Wendy left home when she turned eighteen. She'd not been able to wait for that time to come. At eighteen, she could legally live elsewhere. It had always been my hope that my children would grow to be independent, and I was happy that she was going off to do a university degree in fashion and design. She was a confident and competent young woman. But, to my surprise, she complained that I wasn't upset at her leaving!

Martin had left home a little earlier. After leaving school, he'd studied horticulture while working as a gardener, which he loved. In late 1980 he decided to make another visit to my family in Sydney and then his father's family in Victoria. At a farewell party at our home near York, he told everybody that his wish was to travel the world, make his fortune, buy a plane and fly it back to England! Martin was a much-loved resident of our village of Sutton upon Derwent. He knew everyone, having delivered milk and daily papers during his years there, and by nature being a most sociable person. Many local friends (and his piano teacher from York) packed our large house to wish him 'Bon Voyage'.

This time his flight was uneventful. But what happened next was a bit of a surprise. The day after the plane arrived in Sydney, Martin had a full-time job! He was staying with my mother, and she used her powers of 'gentle persuasion'. He successfully applied for

UNEXPECTED AND UNWELCOME EVENTS

work at the local Woolworths, beginning as a gardening assistant, and in time becoming their produce manager. But in 1986, Martin's love of plants and gardening led him to move on to a full-time job in propagation at a nursery at Glenorie, and to enrolling in further part-time studies in horticulture. He continued to help out at Woolworths on Thursday nights and Saturday mornings.

CHAPTER 11

THINGS OF THE SPIRIT

Some years before Martin or Wendy left home, in 1977, at age forty-two, I was christened for the first time. Neither of my parents had ever been christened, which was unusual at that time (1905 and 1908), and as I mentioned, they'd decided not to have their children affiliated with any religion. They said that once we were fourteen we could decide for ourselves. On forms my father usually described himself as Agnostic or Muhammadan. My mother had an open mind, but was concerned about appearances. She sometimes put C of E. She had, in her youth, attended a Church of England Sunday School. Soon after I started school at OLMC I'd begged my parents to let me be baptised. The nuns were doing their best to convert us.

'Diane, how lovely it will be', said Sister Pascal. 'You can be baptised and take your first Communion in the school chapel. You'll wear a pretty white dress and a white veil'.

THINGS OF THE SPIRIT

I wanted it so badly. But my mother's response was always the same.

'Sweetie, when you're fourteen you can be baptised. Not before'.

Much as I liked the idea of the white dress and veil, my interest went deeper. In religion classes we'd been told of various forms of baptism—baptism of fire (for those who were about to be killed and wished to give their lives to God), baptism of water (the usual one) and baptism of desire (for those not able to have the other kinds). In desperation I performed a do-it-yourself 'baptism of desire' in the shower at home when I was seven or eight.

By age fourteen, however, I had a very different outlook. After seven years at the Catholic school I regarded religion as an unnecessary crutch. We'd been brought up to do the right thing without fear of hell as an incentive. My view at that time was that organised religion was for weak people.

From university days, when my studies included psychology and philosophy, I'd been particularly interested in the big questions. What makes us tick? What are the basic truths of the world's major religions and spiritual practices?

In my early twenties, when Tony and I were practising yoga and were introduced to meditation, we went to a talk on transcendental meditation in Sydney by the Maharishi Mahesh Yogi, and we read about reincarnation, astral travel, levitation, numerology and spiritual healing. Tony was a practising Christian, but was also interested in Eastern spirituality. At the church in Miranda where I'd played the organ, the minister had been extremely judgemental and prejudiced, and at that time his sermons made me a very angry atheist indeed. My views were more aligned with those expressed in one of my favourite books, the 1965 children's book *Many Paths, One Heaven* by Nuri Mass.

By the time I was in my mid-thirties, and teaching music at a top C of E private school, Christianity began to make sense to me in theory. I was attending regular religious services in the school chapel and teaching hymns for the daily assemblies. I 'understood' Christian teachings for the first time.

But it was my marital situation and personal experience in England that led me to the realisation that there really is a power we can call on, something unseen and seemingly greater than us. Throughout my tempestuous seventeen years with Richard, there was a lot of verbal abuse and, at times, incidents of physical violence. We both wanted to be in control, but when unhappy or frustrated we would suppress our emotions until they 'exploded'. I tried everything I could when Richard lost control. There were times when I acted as if nothing had happened. There were times I got into the car and 'ran away'. I tried fighting back. None of these worked, although the running away was the best of the three as it took me out of the situation. I was able to calm myself down and, by the time I returned, Richard had also calmed down and, in fact, was always full of remorse.

THINGS OF THE SPIRIT

But eventually I found a better way, and it surprised me. One night, in the bedroom, about to go to bed, Richard attacked me physically. I immediately silently prayed for him—a simple 'God bless Richard' in my head. He instantly became a different person. I'd found the power of prayer.

So at forty-two, living in this small English village where the church was the heart of the community and the new minister was clearly practising what he preached, I looked afresh at Christianity. I read through the whole of the Bible and came to the conclusion that everything Jesus supposedly said fitted with my beliefs. I decided to become a member of the Church of England, and was duly baptised and confirmed. Wendy and Martin had been christened as soon as we adopted them—it was a legal requirement. Now Wendy decided to be confirmed along with other teenagers (and me).

I was sad but not surprised when Richard refused to attend the service. He'd never been christened. At the time I met him he meditated regularly and had an 'inner voice' that gave him valuable guidance when he tuned in to it. As a composer, he was intuitive. Richard could dream a complete musical composition, which he would notate in the following days. For many years he'd been interested in Buddhism, but he didn't identify with any organised form of spirituality.

After my christening, I was thrilled to be given the key to the church. I enjoyed going there alone, first thing each morning, to silently read a verse at random and meditate on it.

JUST AN ORDINARY PERSON

When Simon turned seven, he asked to be christened, so both he and Graeme had the ceremony together in our local church.

The 'power of praise' was something I discovered during Wendy's pregnancy. Our lovely childbirth preparation teacher had given me a little paperback book, 'Power in Praise' by Merlin R. Carothers, when she first met Wendy. She thought it would help me. And it did. And still does, more than forty years later. The Bible talks about giving thanks and praise at all times, yet I don't think many of us consider saying thank you when things go wrong. The author of this book, a former Navy chaplain, told lots of stories where doing just that worked miracles. His book was full of case studies. He wrote about the couple who learned their daughter was a prostitute, the man whose wife had just left him, and the family living with an alcoholic grandfather. In every instance, this clergyman knelt with the people, and together they thanked God for what had happened. And the changes in those situations were astounding.

I loved this book and decided to put it into practice. I didn't have to wait long. The very next day I was rushing to go to a fundraising event at a neighbour's. I pulled out the drawer where we kept the front door key and the whole drawer came out, spilling all its contents on the floor.

'Thank you, God', I said out loud. And I laughed. It seemed so ridiculous. But as I quickly began putting everything back into the drawer, I found an item I'd been looking for for ages and thought was lost.

THINGS OF THE SPIRIT

On arrival at the event I bought a cake and asked if they'd keep it for me till I was leaving. I also bought tickets in a raffle. The cake seller came to me soon afterwards in a very upset state. Someone had sold my cake, and she was so apologetic. She certainly didn't expect my response of 'Thank you, God'. This was a church-run fundraiser, after all, so it seemed the perfect opportunity to say something about the book and my experience with the drawer, and to explain why I wasn't the least bit upset about losing my cake. The raffle was drawn. I won first prize—the most enormous and beautiful cake I've ever seen.

* * *

The Findhorn Foundation in Scotland played a most important part in my spiritual development. I'd been reading their regular newsletters for some years, and had called in there briefly in 1974 when Richard and I drove with Martin, Wendy and baby Simon to the Scottish island of Eigg for a short self-catering holiday. But at that time and for some years afterwards, I was not financially in a position to do one of their residential courses.

In December 1981, my mother died, quite suddenly, after a heart attack. It was just two days after we'd moved into our newly built house. Before my father's death, he'd set up a family company and allocated shares to all of us—accessible after her death, at which time the company would be wound up. Once the money was distributed, Tina and I and each of our children were comfortable financially. I'd bought a car for myself first thing, and was able to pay for a trip back to Australia with Simon and Graeme, and for some family holidays overseas. Simon and Graeme's money was earning interest in the bank.

So by 1985 I could afford to stay at Findhorn. I vividly recall how I struggled as I wrote to the Foundation to convince them I was worthy of a place. I actually went away from home for a few days in my attempt to cope with giving the required information. I was truly surprised when my application was accepted. Fortunately for everyone, Richard was wonderful with the children whenever I was away, whether they all stayed at home or went on a camping holiday.

From January 1986 to mid-1988 I attended several residential courses at Findhorn. I started with their 'Orientation Week' in early January, and a course in psychic spiritual healing that Easter. I loved being at that beautiful and magical place, and I learned much. During the first week of group games and activities, dancing, cooking and cleaning, a number of people quietly suggested I read *Women Who Love Too Much*. Oops! When I got home I bought the book and read it, and I began to see myself and my great need to love and help others in a new light. I was also told that week that the leader of the Easter healing course was an excellent clairvoyant, and it might be helpful to have a session with her. Always one to open the door fearlessly when opportunity knocks, I made an appointment for a reading during my Easter visit.

At the initial gathering of our healing workshop, we sat in a circle and, in turn, we had to say why we were there. I was there because I was interested in the subject and wanted to learn more about it. I was shocked when we were told that, at the end of the course, each one of us would be giving spiritual healing to members of the public. I contemplated going home. I felt that I was there under false pretences. Everyone else wanted to be a healer.

But I didn't leave. I stayed for the two-week program. Some of our time was spent outdoors meditating in nature. I loved the experience of sitting on a rock by the river and gazing for two hours at a certain spot on a rock in front of me. No one else was around, I was warmly wrapped, and the air was clear and crisp. The north of Scotland can be so beautiful at that time of year, with blue skies and occasional pure white clouds.

I also enjoyed the group activities, such as gathering firewood. We formed a sort of chain gang to move the heavy logs, and chanted in rhythm as we passed the logs to one another. Indoors, we were learning to feel the energy between our hands, did exercises in clairvoyance, recalled past lives (I recalled some with Richard and one with Graeme), and learned techniques for being fully present and connected to the highest energies, disregarding our personal thoughts (monkey mind). By the end, we were all competent and fairly confident.

We worked in groups, taking turns to be the leader, as we did our hands-on healing for strangers. The leader was one who spoke to the 'client' and quietly directed the others where to stand, where to place hands. It was a special and beautiful experience—a win-win situation. For the person receiving, who would lie on a bed covered by a light blanket, it was a time of deep relaxation, while being taken on a guided meditation and receiving lots of 'love energy'. I can't find words to describe how I felt as the 'healer'. Years later, in Australia, when filling in a form that asked 'When are you happiest?' I wrote 'When doing a spiritual healing'.

As soon as I returned to York, a neighbour and close friend asked me to do a healing for a dear friend of hers who was dying of cancer. Since his diagnosis, his family had refused to discuss the illness. He was now in hospital, very alone, very stressed and having difficulty breathing. So I went to the hospital, made my mental preparations and followed my intuition. The man was not conscious, but was struggling to breathe and was quite distressed. With a hand gently on his shoulder, I spoke quietly to him. The 'healing' over, and feeling quite awkward, I silently slipped out of the room and out of the hospital. My friend came to me the next day. She'd visited him after I'd left. He'd been awake and calm. He told her that he felt at peace for the first time. He died in his sleep that night.

That was actually very reassuring for me, as the very next week I was flying to Sydney to be a support person for my sister. Tina had been diagnosed with cancer in most of her bones. She wanted to attend a weeklong course in Victoria run by Ian Gawler for people with cancer. She and her husband had grown apart since her diagnosis, and Tina asked me if I could possibly go there with her. She'd be in a wheelchair and needed someone to accompany her.

I flew over from England to Australia, and during the flight I managed to read an excellent book written for families of people with cancer. Tina had recommended it to me. She'd bought a copy in the hope that her husband would read it. This book not only helped me know how best to help her, it also gave me insights into what the rest of the family were probably experiencing. I had a long talk the first night with my brother-in-law, and told him quite a bit about what was in the book. He stopped being defensive. On our return from Victoria, Tina was happily surprised to find that he'd read the book thoroughly and was now relaxed and supportive. From then until her death more than two years later, their relationship was back on track.

She and I very much enjoyed that time away together. We'd always been close, and I'd been living overseas for fourteen years. One night during the week at the cancer clinic, as she was lying in bed ready for sleep, Tina unburdened herself of a 'guilt' she'd been carrying for twenty years. She'd been blaming herself for the fact that her youngest son was mentally handicapped. She told me she had eaten fish and chips one day during her pregnancy—she was a vegetarian. I stroked her forehead as she cried and began to let go of her long-held pain.

The fact of the matter was that she'd previously had a miscarriage. Her doctor had made the decision to surgically prevent a further miscarriage as soon as another pregnancy was confirmed. This was done—the cervix was stitched—but for months before her third son was born, her body tried to abort. In the last weeks she was hospitalised and heavily sedated to stop labour occurring. No one was really surprised that this baby was 'different'.

* * *

JUST AN ORDINARY PERSON

The clairvoyant reading I had during the spiritual healing course in 1986 was one of my life-changing events. I remember Carol, the workshop leader, telling us that the most difficult part of clairvoyant reading is selecting what will be most helpful to the person being read. Well, she certainly selected the most appropriate bit of information to pass on to me. And she recorded everything she said on tape, so I was able to listen to it again and again.

'All your life you have been trying hard to please others. First your mother, then your husbands'. 'You have a right to be you. Just as you are'.

She said I was to stop putting myself out in order to do what others expected of me—or what I thought they expected of me. It wouldn't be easy to make the change, but I needed to do it. She said she could see Richard 'falling flat on his face' when I stopped trying to help him. But I would be there to help him up. It would benefit us both.

OMG! I'd not realised before that trying to help others can actually weaken them and lead to them resenting you for it. Anyway, I went home. I even played the tape to Richard, though he made no response—it was as if he hadn't heard it. I was full of determination to speak up for myself when appropriate, and to put Carol's advice into practice. I soon had the opportunity.

Richard rushed into the kitchen one morning a few days after my return.

THINGS OF THE SPIRIT

'My battery's flat! I'll have to take your car today'. I took a deep breath. My heart was in my mouth.

'I've arranged to drive to York today for shopping. I—I could take you in later. Why not ring the AA (Automobile Association) and have them come and start the car?'

Richard wasn't happy, but he made the call, they came and started his car, and off he went. The incident wasn't mentioned again.

But the next day the same thing happened.

'Dee, the battery's flat again. I'll just ring the AA.'

Believe it or not, the following day I looked out the window to see an AA man starting Richard's car. Richard hadn't even told me about his third (and final) flat battery.

And so it was that I helped less and my husband became more independent. But living with him was still stressful, and I looked forward to the times when I could get away, or his work took him away from home. One such time was his visit to the USA for the performance of a commissioned musical composition. As usual, Richard had not completed the work on time. He ended up writing sections and posting them to America for the performers to learn. The day he was to leave York, the piece was still unfinished. He'd been composing early mornings at home, and I pointed out that he could get up early the next morning in London, before his flight, and finish it then. He decided to do that.

Richard had previously agreed to my suggestion that he order a taxi to take him to the train rather than have me drive him there. And thank God he did. That morning he was in such a flap. A call from upstairs:

'Dee, I need your help. I can't get my vest on'. I went up and helped. The taxi was outside. Richard wasn't dressed. He had no idea where his passport was.

I heaved a sigh of relief after his departure (with passport). Previously I would have packed everything for him. I would have had his passport and tickets at the ready, his clothes laid out. I'd done nothing, yet his parting words, sincerely meant, were, 'You've been so helpful'.

That night I slept soundly. But it was like a bad dream when the phone rang at 6:30 am with a frantic Richard on the line.

'I'm coming home!'

He was in a phone box in the middle of London. He was in a terrible state. He'd lost the key to his suitcase, and hadn't been able to unlock it to finish writing the music. No locksmiths were open. He couldn't face the people in America. He was cancelling his flight. He was on the way home. I could hear the noisy city traffic in the background.

The impact of his first words ('I'm coming home') had sent the adrenaline flowing fast in me. My immediate thought—no, 'de-

THINGS OF THE SPIRIT

termination' describes it better—was 'No way!' I didn't consciously call on unseen helpers, but I found myself speaking quietly and soothingly, calming his agitation. I pointed out that he could still travel as planned, have the case unlocked in Cleveland, and finish off the composition the following morning. There were still several days before the performance.

'Phone me from the airport once you're booked in,' I told him. And I held my breath. He mumbled something and ended the call.

Every bit of me was visualising him going to the airport. But I was so nervous after he'd hung up. I had no idea what he would do. Fortunately for everyone, Richard caught the plane. He did phone me from the London terminal to say he had checked in and was ready to board the flight. And he called me after arrival in Cleveland. All was well. His colleague had arranged for a locksmith to open the case and was fine with everything.

That afternoon I received another call from America. A radio station there wanted to interview me about what it was like to be married to a composer. I laughed, before I went on to make the arrangements for their representative to visit and record me the next day. (I didn't tell them that story.)

CHAPTER 12

MAJOR CHANGES AND NEW OPPORTUNITIES

*I*n 1988, English TV was full of Australia's bicentennial celebrations. My sister's health was deteriorating. She'd hoped to be well enough to visit England, and had arranged to spend a week with me in London while her husband was on a business trip to the continent. But the cancer had spread to her brain. Tina phoned me to say she was in hospital, and the trip would have to be postponed. I immediately said I'd visit her. Graeme wanted to come, too. He had a close bond with Tina and offered to pay for himself. I booked for us both on the next possible plane.

My older son Martin had now been back in Australia some eight years—he was twenty-eight. He'd recently done well in the annual 'City to Surf' fourteen-kilometre running event, and was keen to show me a newspaper clipping about it. Martin planned to

MAJOR CHANGES AND NEW OPPORTUNITIES

meet us at Sydney airport at 6 am and drive us to my sister's home, where we would stay.

Our plane landed, but there was no sign of Martin. We phoned Tina's husband, and one of my nephews collected us. We then got a call to say that Martin had been seriously injured in a car accident late the night before. He'd suffered severe brain damage as well as broken ribs, and was in a coma—in the same intensive-care ward as my sister!

It was extraordinary. To add to the coincidences, the nurse looking after Martin knew him from school in Pocklington, England. And my brother-in-law had a work colleague in that same intensive-care ward, so when he visited, he was there to see his wife, his nephew and his friend from work. I was there for my son and my sister. There was a small waiting room for visitors, and that area became a social centre for our family and friends. In fact, the hospital provided so many amenities that Graeme and I also had our hair cut, did our banking there and, of course, we had lunch at the hospital most days. I had the use of my brother-in-law's car, and was able to drive to Martin's written-off car, empty it and make the necessary arrangements on his behalf, as well as making the daily trips to and from the hospital.

Once Martin and Tina were moved to other wards, more visitors were allowed. But my son was still in a coma.

On hearing of the accident and Martin's condition, some close friends of his (and ours) in York made a tape recording on which they spoke to Martin. Through their local radio station, they tracked down someone who was about to fly to Sydney. They got the tape to that person, and it reached us at the hospital. Once Martin was connected to the cassette player with earphones, we watched as there was the first sign of an expression on his face. We replayed their message to him many times—and Martin came out of his six-week coma.

His physical health was good, as he'd been in excellent health previously. Mentally, we were told that permanent damage between the left and right hemispheres of his brain would mean he would never be able to live alone, work or drive. In those days it was believed that brain cells could not regenerate or be replaced but, that with rehabilitation, he would be able to learn to walk and talk, use money, etc. Martin was moved to another hospital for months of rehab.

During one of my conversations with Tina's husband, I told him of how painful my relationship with Richard was, and I was somewhat surprised when he said, 'If it's like that, why do you stay with him?'

For so long I'd not had the money to consider leaving Richard, but I now realised that leaving would be possible. I decided that, if on my return, things were as bad as before, then I would leave him and return to Australia.

So I went back to York with a new viewpoint and a feeling of empowerment. Life went on as before, but now I knew that I had

MAJOR CHANGES AND NEW OPPORTUNITIES

the option of being free of Richard's control and the seemingly unsolvable problems in our relationship. I told no one, but I soon decided that I was not willing to continue living this way. I quietly made all the arrangements to return to Australia with Simon and Graeme.

When at last I told Richard, and discussed with him selling the house we jointly owned, he responded three ways. At first, he more or less laughed at me. 'You'll change your mind and stay', he said confidently.

Then, as time went on and he realised I was serious, he announced that he would not sign any papers regarding the sale of the house. If I left, it would be without that money.

Only after I'd continued with the arrangements and made public the fact that the boys and I were returning to Australia did Richard accept the separation was inevitable. He signed the papers, and the house was sold. He made arrangements to move to university accommodation, where he lived until well after his retirement.

Fortunately we parted as friends. Richard drove us to the coach station, and we travelled by bus to London. Simon, Graeme and I stayed there at a hotel overnight and had breakfast with Wendy before heading to the airport. Wendy had completed her arts degree in fashion design and was now living in London, the city of her choice.

JUST AN ORDINARY PERSON

My sister's cancer had worsened during the three months I'd been back in England. She died a few days before we left. We arrived in time for her funeral.

* * *

Graeme had always been the peacemaker in our family. From a very young age he'd had the ability to sit quietly and 'ask God' for advice. This started before I discovered how to connect to my own inner voice/higher self. The worst times for our family had been university holidays and weekends, when Richard was at home all day. I remember one Christmas period when things were really bad.

'Graeme, will you ask God what we should do?' I asked in desperation. Graeme sat down, closed his eyes, then wrote out a detailed plan of family activities for the next few days. We followed them, and it was probably the happiest time we'd had together.

Graeme was thirteen when he learned I was leaving Richard. He felt he'd failed. He begged us to stay together. 'Mummy, you and Dad have been getting on so well recently', he pointed out to me. It was true. Once I was no longer trying to make the relationship work, I was much happier, and the last few months had been a period of comparative calm. But I never doubted my decision. I was convinced I was doing the right thing by leaving.

Simon, Graeme and I returned to a very wet Sydney in early December 1988. This time, a recovering Martin was with the family members who met us at the airport. Initially we stayed at my sister's place and went with the rest of her family to her funeral. It was

MAJOR CHANGES AND NEW OPPORTUNITIES

especially nice for me to reunite with distant family and friends that day.

Martin was ready to leave the rehab hospital, so I straight away looked for a furnished rental property close to where he would be having further daytime rehabilitation. I found the perfect place for us all at Willoughby. I bought a car, because my previous one could not be brought to Australia as that model and its parts were not available here. I bought a piano—a Disklavier. It's a standard piano but with a built-in computer, allowing recording and automatic playing of disks. Like a pianola, it can play 'by itself', the keys and pedals moving up and down. I also went to Ikea and bought an extra bed and some bookshelves. Richard and I had amicably decided who would have what of our household belongings, but mine had been packed into shipping containers and were coming by sea.

And so we settled nicely into our new and quite spacious apartment. Martin, Simon and Graeme shared the largest bedroom. Martin was picked up by car most days and taken to rehab. His memory loss was such that he would ask the same question over and over again, having no awareness that he'd already asked it and received an answer. It was a lesson in patience for us. More difficult was dealing with his purchases. He negotiated to buy a complete lounge, dining and bedroom suite of beautiful antique furniture. I had to get a solicitor involved to get him out of that one. The smaller items, which I usually found under his bed, I would return to the shops he'd bought them from.

JUST AN ORDINARY PERSON

Since his accident Martin thought every girl who spoke to him—or sent a card when he was in hospital—wanted to marry him. He was obsessed with thinking about which of them he would choose. And he wanted to start a horticultural business. It wasn't long before our large balcony was absolutely covered in plants that Martin had propagated from cuttings.

Simon and Graeme, who were by now fourteen and fifteen, easily adapted to the major changes in their schooling, and soon made new friends—all, like them, from overseas. Graeme continued his piano and trombone studies and was able to play in his school's top class concert band. Simon continued his violin studies. I considered working, and even applied for a job at the university as a guide. But I now had enough money to stay at home. I'd decided never to teach piano again, as that had been Richard's decision, not mine. As much as I enjoyed it, I wanted to freely make my own choices.

I still felt the need to improve myself and to help others, so I enrolled in a two-year, part-time course in counselling and psychotherapy. I also trained as a counsellor with the Child Abuse Prevention Service. And I sang again with the Sydney University Graduate Choir of which I was a life member.

After nine months, Martin was offered accommodation through the rehabilitation centre. He had the opportunity to live in an assisted-living house with three other young men—all of whom had some kind of disability. After much discussion, it was decided that Martin would take up the offer and move from our place. In

MAJOR CHANGES AND NEW OPPORTUNITIES

addition to the new accommodation, arrangements were made for him to work at a nearby Woolworths supermarket. Three years previously he'd been a manager in the fruit and vegetable department of one of their stores. Now the one nearest to him was paid to let him work there as part of his rehabilitation. Thirty years later, Martin is still working for Woolworths. He has received an award for outstanding customer service, and has shared his enthusiasm for life (and his favourite recipes) with many of the people he has served. In the past three years I've accompanied Martin on three short cruises and, on every one of them, we've met up with customers who sing his praises!

Martin's accommodation has changed, however. After leaving the assisted housing, he managed to live alone in two rented places and as a lodger in a beautiful home close to his work. Then for some years he lived with his elderly 'step-granny', his stepmother Marianne's mother. He was with her until she was 103, and he stayed in her house caring for her dog when she then moved to a nursing home for a year before her death. After her house was sold, he moved back to the room he'd previously lodged in, overlooking Middle Harbour. Martin was included in his step-granny's will—a wonderful bonus as he approaches retirement.

* * *

In late 1989, once Martin was happily settled and being cared for in the assisted-living house, Simon, Graeme and I jointly bought a house in Katoomba in the Blue Mountains.

JUST AN ORDINARY PERSON

It was strange! I hadn't thought about buying a house or moving. I had attended a weekend workshop run by author and healer Edmund Harold in Leura, near Katoomba. The next morning I realised I'd left my toiletries behind. It was a lovely day and I had no commitments, so I decided to drive back there and collect them. I stopped at Glenbrook for petrol and to get a map of the mountains area. As I walked into the service station, I noticed a pile of local newspapers. On the front page was a photograph and an ad for a house for sale in Katoomba. It was affordable if the three of us combined our inheritance money. It drew me. I picked up the paper and drove to Leura. After collecting my toiletries, I went straight to the estate agent's and bought the house.

Before moving, I made many trips to Katoomba. I painted the front door and all of the interior. I had woodweave blinds made for all the windows and a beautiful new kitchen installed. Simon was sixteen and about to start his final year at school. His teachers strongly advised that he stay in Sydney so as not to change schools again. So he boarded with one of his classmates, and spent weekends and school holidays with Graeme and me at Katoomba.

Richard came over from England every Christmas, and usually spent some weeks with us. The first visit, just twelve months after I'd left him, I was feeling quite stressed in advance, and I developed some stiffness and joint pain the week before he arrived. We all reconnected harmoniously. Richard and I even had thoughts of us buying a larger house with a swimming pool, and all living together again in Australia. Simon and Graeme were both hoping we would reunite, and loved the idea.

MAJOR CHANGES AND NEW OPPORTUNITIES

I'd been cleaning house once a week for Edmund Harold, who then lived near Springwood. I told him what we were considering. At that stage, we'd not divorced. Edmund did a 'reading' for me.

'I see you and Richard being the best of friends', he said. 'But too close, no'. He said much more about the dynamic between us and of past life experiences. I decided to take his advice.

***

At Katoomba, when he was fifteen, Graeme became addicted to playing arcade games. He was very good at them, and even won a competition at the local venue. But in school holidays he would go there at opening time and would not be able to leave until they shut at night. I remember him returning home later than planned one night, and entering through his bedroom window.

'I felt terrible about it', he told me. 'I couldn't stop playing'.

Since we'd left England, Graeme's relationship with me had been close, but often volatile. He was, in many ways, a miniature version of his father. It seemed I was dealing with similar dynamics to those I'd left behind. Graeme began making the worst choices. He was with young friends one day when they messed around on a building site and a fire was started. Graeme claimed one of the younger boys was responsible but, being the oldest, he got the blame. It was his first encounter with the police. I was with him at the police station where he was fingerprinted and charged. There was a court hearing and Graeme was found guilty but no conviction recorded.

JUST AN ORDINARY PERSON

Around this time I was surprised to find one of my bras was torn. Graeme admitted to trying it on. I thought this might have been normal teenage behaviour—but years later I was to learn that Graeme was happiest dressed in women's clothing and living as a woman. He was only ever attracted to the opposite sex, though, and he often expressed the hope of marrying and having children.

Graeme was always wanting to be back in England. He missed his father, his school friends, his cousins, uncles and aunts. In his final year at Katoomba High School, with no idea of what he wanted to do with his life, and with his relationship with me being so difficult at times, we agreed that it might be best if he went back and lived with Richard. We found out he could sit his Higher School Certificate exams as a distance student from England. So after discussing it with Richard, the flight was booked. I made the necessary arrangements with the Education Department, and Graeme flew to London.

Once he was with his father in York, Graeme quickly met up with his old school friends, now a few miles away, and was terribly disappointed. They'd all 'moved on' during the four years he'd been away. And his being with his father wasn't what he'd expected, either. Graeme hardly did any school work, which led to many arguments. He and Richard had never got on very well together—in some ways they were too alike, and in some ways they were too different. With much inconvenience to all concerned, a good friend of Richard's supervised Graeme as he sat all his HSC exams at the time of the Australian ones—some in the middle of the night. Then just two days after the final exam, Graeme was back

MAJOR CHANGES AND NEW OPPORTUNITIES

in Australia. The grass was not greener on the other side. He'd changed his mind soon after arriving in the UK and, as soon as he could leave, he did. Graeme returned to our home in Katoomba.

***

I had now completed a course in permaculture with the wonderful, world-renowned teacher Rosemary Morrow. I'd also trained as an announcer with the local community radio station, and interviewed Rosemary in a 'Desert Island Discs'-type program as part of that training. (But, unlike my mother, I hadn't pursued that line of work.)

Our permaculture studies had introduced us to alternative trading systems, and a group of us decided to set one up. The Blue Mountains Local Exchange and Trading System (LETS) became the largest in the world. At that time people were not able to use the internet. The members would phone me to say what goods or services they were offering or wanted, and what transactions had taken place. I used to carry a 'modern' cordless phone, notepad and pen in a bag around my waist. Whether I was gardening in the beautiful permaculture beds designed by me and set up by our class, or doing things inside the house, I was at the ready. I would periodically go to the home of another committee member to enter the data into her Mac computer (we only had a PC, and the LETS software had been designed for a Mac). The list of offers and requests was regularly printed out and distributed. I got to know all of the members, and enjoyed very much contributing to the success of this venture.

JUST AN ORDINARY PERSON

And I was able to benefit greatly in a practical way. Through this form of 'bartering', I had a most beautiful room added across the back of our house. A LETS architect designed it, and all the building work was done by LETS members. I arranged for people to cook delicious food for the workers. New curtains were sewn, and some new furniture 'bought' through the system.

There was a big act of faith involved, however. I remember a friend saying to me, 'You mustn't commit yourself until you have the money for the materials'. I had no idea where the money for the wood, glass and cement, etc., would come from, but I had a sense it would be forthcoming. I no longer had any capital and, having found I was eligible for a sole-parent pension, was now living from one Centrelink payment to the next. Following my gut, I placed the orders for all the necessary materials. When Richard learned of my plans, he offered to pay a year's child support for the boys, in advance, in one lump sum. It was exactly the amount I needed.

To get LETS currency to pay the members for all their work, I sold everything of use that I didn't want. I traded down my washing machine, I 'sold' a beautiful tapestry I was never going to sew, I did lots of babysitting, I cleaned house and, of course, I earned LETS 'dollars' with my administrative work.

The stiffness and joint pain I experienced a couple of months after the move to Katoomba, become arthritis. There were times it was so severe that I physically couldn't lift the doona off myself in the mornings. I couldn't use a knife or tin opener. My hands, wrists and feet were badly affected and, in time, became misshapen. I read

MAJOR CHANGES AND NEW OPPORTUNITIES

a number of books on natural treatments for arthritis, and made some improvements to my diet. And I visited the Hopewood Health Centre at Mulgoa, a place I'd been to for an annual fast years earlier when living in Miranda and Wahroonga. They used sunshine, fresh air, water, wholesome vegetarian food, juices and fasts as therapies. When I'd first joined the Natural Health Society some twenty-seven years earlier, and was studying naturopathy, I'd undertaken a lengthy 'fast' while at home for the benefit of my physical and spiritual health. For sixteen days I had nothing but water when thirsty, then watered-down juices for another five. It had been an enjoyable and most beneficial experience.

After this latest stay at Hopewood I was much improved. During the months that followed I also had some spiritual healing with Edmund Harold, and a number of sessions with a hypnotherapist trained in hypnoanalysis—all of which was most helpful.

In January 1992, Richard and I were divorced. I made all the arrangements from my end, and attended the courthouse in Parramatta.

In late 1992, I read that the NSW Government was funding a twelve-month job in the Hunter Valley for a LETS Community Officer. The successful applicant would be based in Newcastle and travel throughout the Hunter area giving public talks about the benefits of LETSystems, and setting them up in all the large towns. Apart from my admin and personal experience in our local system, I'd met and done training with Michael Linton, the Canadian expert on LETS, and I'd given talks to groups such as the Blue Mountains

JUST AN ORDINARY PERSON

Chamber of Commerce. I decided to apply, and I got the job. I immediately had a number of computer lessons with a Blue Mountains LETS member, so as to better understand the software I'd be introducing to others.

CHAPTER 13

MANY MOVES AND MUCH ACTIVITY

From March 1993 to March 1994, I lived at New Lambton Heights near Newcastle, NSW. Graeme, now aged eighteen, stayed on at our Katoomba house and worked at the checkout of the local Franklin's supermarket. Simon had stayed in Sydney after leaving school, and was living in rented accommodation. He'd won a scholarship to do an Advanced Science degree at the University of NSW in Kensington. By the time I left Katoomba, Simon was in his final year of studies and playing the violin in the university orchestra.

My new accommodation was with a Newcastle LETS member. He was the treasurer of the committee that would supervise my work for the year. I lodged underneath his house in a good-sized room with a bed and plenty of desk area. My very small TV sat on a shelf suspended from the ceiling. There was an adjoining shower room and toilet for my use. My piano moved with me and was conveniently housed in the double garage, which was my main entry. My landlord and I got on well, and from time to time socialised together.

For my new job a computer and printer were provided, and also a large book in which I was to record each night what I had done that day. This was somewhat time-consuming, and it was probably the part of the job I liked least. I seemed to spend so much time just recording where I'd been, what I'd done, the mileage in my car, the phone calls, the correspondence in and out, and the individual costs of everything I bought. But it was an essential requirement. Each month the book was checked when I met with the overseeing committee to present my written, printed report, and receive reimbursement for necessary expenses. My work logs were done with fountain pen.

At 'home' in my super-efficient office area, I would contact the councils of the towns I wanted to visit. Maitland, Cessnock, Musselbrook, Scone and Quirindi were the main ones on my list. I would arrange to hold a public meeting in a hall, then do the advertising for it, sending information and posters to the council and the local papers. (I had fun using Publisher to create the posters.) On the day of the public meeting I'd drive to the town, set up a display, give my talk, show a short video, answer questions and then conduct a less formal group discussion. Quite often the people attending were strangers, but by the end of the session they'd be enthusiastically arranging for transactions with one another.

MANY MOVES AND MUCH ACTIVITY

It's extraordinary how many of us undervalue ourselves. I found that sitting people in a circle and having them begin to speak about what they wanted or would like would invariably lead to someone else saying:

'I could do that for you!'

'I could provide you with that!' People who thought they had no skills realised they could sew, knit, drive someone to an appointment or babysit. As part of my display, I had large laminated 'before and after' photographs of my Katoomba house extension so people could see that there was no limit to the ways they could benefit through LETS.

New systems were set up in every town I visited, and I would go back to spend time with those who had stepped up to do the admin work, and to keep on eye on their progress.

I thrived in this situation. The job and its varied activities and interactions with people brought out the best in me. And when the twelve months was over, I had saved enough money from my earnings to make a trip back to England to see family and friends and make another visit to Findhorn.

I decided to sell the Katoomba house. Simon, Graeme and I had each contributed a third of the money to purchase it, so the property was owned by us equally. I contacted a Blue Mountains LETS friend who was a real estate agent, and the house was sold—at the price we'd paid for it! House prices had fallen during the five years we'd been there. I'd put a lot of money into the new kitchen and the extension, and expected to receive more than a third of the sale price. However, when it was time to sign the contract, Graeme refused to sign unless he got exactly one-third. He was most unpleasant about it. He told me I'd have to go to court to get him to sign for less.

The idea of doing battle with my son in court was not acceptable to me. I saw no option but to accept Graeme's terms. Simon actually handled the distribution of the money to our accounts, and I did end up with some extra. But it was a most uncomfortable experience. It definitely added to the resentment I had within me.

With the sale completed, most of my household contents went into storage in Newcastle, Graeme went to live with Simon in his flat at Kensington, and I went overseas. Richard's home in York was my headquarters, and while there I learned that Michael Linton was starting up a major LETS initiative in Manchester. He invited me to join the team working on this new project. It was to be unpaid work at first, but with the expectation of generous payments later. Our food and accommodation would be provided. I was most happy to accept the offer.

Michael still lived in Canada, but he had rented a very large residential building in Manchester for himself and those of us who were not local. He'd also rented and equipped offices in the inner city for us to all to work from. I was living and sharing with strangers—something I'd never done before, having moved directly from home to marriage. In the Manchester house we each had a very large, well-appointed bedroom-cum-sitting room. There were

MANY MOVES AND MUCH ACTIVITY

shared kitchens and bathrooms on each floor, and a large dining room and lounge area on the ground floor. We made up a roster for the cleaning of the communal areas, and I used to organise all the evening meals. We were all members of Manchester LETS, so I arranged for various local members to do the catering for us, paying them the cost of the ingredients only. They cooked and delivered the food each day, and we ate very well!

On one memorable occasion, Michael offered our spare rooms to overseas people who were visiting Manchester for a four-day conference. I'm not sure what the conference was about but, next thing I knew, I was welcoming, feeding and entertaining the Russian Minister for Education and an equally high-ranking professional woman—neither of whom spoke English! I don't speak Russian, but she and I got on famously. We drew our children's names and ages on paper serviettes, and had lots of laughs. But it was he who gave me a most cherished 'thank you' present when they left. Hand-crafted in Russia, it's a small round container with lid—most beautifully carved and decorated. I've always loved it and treasured it.

The project itself was a big disappointment. Not a penny was coming in, and with rents, office supplies, advertising, phone bills, and food using all the available resources, LETS Go Manchester eventually folded. We'd all been promised thousands of pounds at the end of the project, but everyone involved ended up out of pocket. There was sadness and frustration about the whole situation, as some of us were aware of the cause of the problems but unable to do anything about it.

JUST AN ORDINARY PERSON

Because of the stresses of the job, I made sure that when back in the house I was relaxed and calm. I was sprouting alfalfa seeds on my sunny windowsill, eating the healthiest of foods, and meditating and doing yoga exercises every day. It was a rich experience for me in many ways, and I formed some strong friendships. A Tasmanian LETS administrator and I bonded and were able to support one another during the difficult times. He fell in love with one of the Manchester people we met through LETS, and often invited me to accompany him as he courted his new love. And I later went back to attend their wedding.

Before returning to Australia, I attended another Findhorn workshop in Scotland. It was a training in leading workshops. It seemed just what I needed, as I'd already completed 'The Art of Living in Peace', a course which trained its participants to 'teach' this most interesting and important material to others. I now felt confident about running workshops in the future.

Having sold the Katoomba house, and with everything in storage, I had the freedom to live anywhere when I returned to Australia in late 1994. A former Blue Mountains resident and close friend, Barbara S, was living in Canberra. In fact, I'd organised LETS members to do the packing and cleaning of her house at the time of her move there, and I'd driven her dog 330 kilometres from Katoomba to Canberra as a LETS transaction! Barbara invited me to stay with her while I found somewhere to live permanently in the ACT, the Australian Capital Territory—the very small area where

MANY MOVES AND MUCH ACTIVITY

the Federal Capital is situated. This territory (and the city of Canberra) is not in New South Wales, though it is within the state of NSW.

I'd visited Canberra before and liked this unusual city. Other Australian cities had just 'grown', but Canberra had been designed. After it was decided to place Australia's capital on this site, there'd been a competition open to architects all over the world. 'Kamberra' was the settlement's Aboriginal name. The word means 'meeting place', and it's thought that thousands of Australia's first people used to come together in that area to hunt and enjoy its resources and seasonal foods.

In 1912 the design of American architect Marion Mahony Griffin was chosen from 136 entries. Her architect husband, Walter Burley Griffin, had submitted the design in his name. This design was reworked by a government committee, who added elements from other plans. The result was 'a real mosaic of ill-fitting puzzle pieces', according to a leading architect at the time. Griffin was furious, and he petitioned the Australian government to bring him here so he could explain his vision. They did but, as happened later with Sydney's famous Opera House, the combination of architect and government bureaucrats was unworkable. Griffin ended up resigning, and the original plans were not fully realised.

However, Canberra, with its wide streets and circular roads, is attractive and distinctive. I enjoyed living there. For the first eighteen months I lived in Ainslie, close to natural bushland and kangaroos. Rabbits ran across my lawn, yet I was a five-minute drive from big department stores and concert venues. I joined the Canberra LETSystem and had my rented half-house painted inside, new shelving made for books, and a no-dig permaculture garden quickly built and planted—all with the help of LETS members. On my block there were established grapevines and productive plum and fig trees. The building was eventually to be pulled down and town houses built, so when I asked the owner for permission to paint and make a garden, she replied, 'Dee, you can do anything you like, except remove the walls!' And I did. I turned it into a most comfortable and beautiful home.

Once I was settled, I began making arrangements to run the workshops on 'The Art of Living in Peace'. After contacting a few people (which included having a personal meeting with a top politician) and preparing my material, I practised some of the presentation with my friend Barbara. I can't recall just what she said, but I do remember that her few quiet words to me afterwards led me to realise that running this workshop was not what I was really wanting to do.

Soon afterwards, I enrolled in yet another lengthy 'self-development' course. I enjoyed the often-challenging classes, and managed to give quite an impressive address on stage to a large audience at the end. I still have strong memories of one of the exercises we did. We had to write down what we were thinking every fifteen minutes, when awake, for a whole week. I found that every thought I recorded was a 'negative' one—anxiety over what I'd wear, what I'd say, what food I'd prepare for a visitor. I was amazed. But I told myself, 'This is not how I usually am. These thoughts are only because at present there's a lot on my plate and a friend is coming to stay'.

But, looking back, I realise that my mind was continually dwelling on possible problems, and I was not the happy and 'together' person I thought I was and that others perceived me to be.

Another piece of homework in this course made a big impression on me. This exercise gave me a new perspective on 'integrity'. On prepared forms, we recorded our thoughts, our words and our actions in regard to dozens of issues. We were told that integrity is when the answers match. Years later I wrote some verses intended for children. This is one of them.

THOUGHT, WORD AND DEED

What we think and what we say
and what we end up doing,
need to be in harmony
if peace we are pursuing.

So only think of what you want,
and watch what you are saying.
Follow through on what you do—
there's no point in delaying.

Integrity is when our thoughts
and words and deeds are matching.
It means we're whole, we're on a roll!
And hopefully it's catching.

JUST AN ORDINARY PERSON

During my years in Canberra, I turned sixty and got a Seniors Card. I also did some overseas travelling. My daughter Wendy, still living in London, decided to get married in Hawaii. She and her fiancé Paul and most of their friends were doing a one-week workshop there prior to the date chosen for the ceremony. Paul offered to pay for my accommodation at their hotel, the Ritz Carlton on Maui, for that week. I paid for my flights, and for an excursion by coach around the island.

It was a most wonderful week for me, and the outdoor wedding was beautiful and filled with love. We were all dressed entirely in white, apart from the special flower leis put around our necks as we arrived—a symbol of affection. Wendy looked stunning in the dress she had designed and made herself. Paul, in his all-white outfit, was equally outstanding and handsome. Everything was 'picture perfect'. My happy memories of the event will always be with me.

In April 1996, I travelled to London and stayed with Wendy and Paul for the birth of their daughter. It was lovely being there for those weeks, sharing their joyful experiences and getting to know Paul's mother. Wendy and Paul lived in a one-bedroom flat in Notting Hill, so I slept in the living room with their cockatoo, which was quite an experience. Eros was 'one of the family', and a rather disruptive one. He usually lived outside of his large and expensive Harrods cage during the day, flying at speed from one end of the flat to the other, being fed his own little bowl of porridge at the kitchen table, and having his beak brushed with a small toothbrush. Much of the time he chewed away at the timber window frames. Wendy has always loved birds and animals. At the time, she also

MANY MOVES AND MUCH ACTIVITY

had a cat and a dog. All three pets attended homeopathic practitioners when unwell.

* * *

Richard continued to visit Australia each Christmas, and we often spent it at a lovely holiday home belonging to a Blue Mountains LETS friend. It was on the Central Coast in a tiny beachside town, which was very quiet and beautiful and close to national parkland where we enjoyed many bush walks. Simon, Graeme and Martin joined us whenever they could. We always spent a very happy Christmas Day together.

Richard would never holiday alone, and for many years he paid for me to fly to England to go on holiday with him. We did trips to Ireland, to the Canadian Rockies, and three trips to different resorts in Turkey. They were very happy times. We were comfortable in our platonic relationship, though I later learned that Richard was still hoping we'd remarry.

Before I moved to Canberra, I'd made a good friend in Newcastle. She is still a close friend and has played a major role in my life during the past twenty-five years. The way we met was unusual. I was attending a talk, and got into conversation with the woman sitting beside me. I can't recall what we were speaking about, but she said, 'You must meet Judy M'. And she wrote down and gave me the name and phone number. Judy was a psychologist, and at that time was working as a financial advisor. I made an appointment to see her at her office—and that began a deep and lasting friendship.

Richard usually arrived in Australia for his Christmas visit at the beginning of December, as both Graeme and Martin had early-December birthdays and we would all celebrate them together. Judy's birthday is mid-December. One year when Richard was visiting, he accompanied me on the drive from Canberra to Newcastle when I travelled there for Judy's birthday party. I'd been invited to stay the weekend at her place, and Richard intended dropping me off and staying at a motel. However, on arrival, I introduced Judy to Richard, and she insisted he stay as well. It was a wonderful weekend. The best 'house-party', with her daughter and son-in-law staying there, too. The first night, Judy and I sat together long after everyone else had gone to bed and talked and talked. I think it was about three o'clock when we ended our conversation and got to bed.

We had further long, 'deep and meaningful' conversations when she visited Canberra a couple of times while I was there, and we kept in touch. When Judy told me she was considering going to live in the north-west country town of Barraba, halfway between Tamworth and Moree, and was thinking of building a number of yurts there, I was really interested. I loved the idea of living in a yurt. Judy invited me to join her for the trip, so I drove to Newcastle then joined her for the drive to Barraba. As we approached the town, passing the tall silos (now beautifully painted by artist Fintan Magee) I felt such a pull—like a tug at my heart. I wanted to live there. Yurt or no yurt, I decided I would move to Barraba. I would find a rental property there.

MANY MOVES AND MUCH ACTIVITY

I told Richard of my plans when I next wrote to him, and to my amazement and delight he offered to buy a house there, of my choosing, which I could rent from him. He'd decided to take early retirement from his university lecturing job and was about to receive a large lump sum.

And so I made a second trip to Barraba, this time by train and coach. I was thinking about what I wanted in a house. I definitely wanted a bath, and preferably a separate shower. And I wanted a large garden so I could have lots of fruit trees as well as veggie and herb gardens. I didn't mention my concerns to the little old woman sitting quietly beside me on the train, though I did tell her, when she boarded, that I was on my way to buy a house. As she left the train, she surprised me with her parting words: 'Follow your heart, not your head'.

On arrival in Barraba I met up with the estate agent I'd previously contacted, and he drove me to inspect a number of houses. (There was no online house-hunting at that time.) As we turned into a short, dead-end street to see the last house on his list, my body reacted strangely. I can't describe it in words. But I remember I couldn't speak. I was sort of choked up, emotionally. My eyes watered and my nose ran. Seconds later we reached the house, and I immediately knew it would be perfect for me. This was another Pettit and Sevitt white-painted brick house, with a bath and a separate shower and a wood-burning stove. It was 'split level' with three bedrooms and a toilet up a short flight of stairs. And there was an enormous backyard for fruit and veggie growing. I went straight from the agent's office to the local solicitor's, where the sale was set in motion.

Prior to my moving to Barraba, Richard came over to sign the legal papers. There was a brief hitch when the solicitor realised that, since we were no longer married, Richard could not legally own a house in Australia unless he was living in it. So the purchase was made in Simon's name (and Simon eventually bought it from his father).

Richard shopped with me for furniture and fittings, and he paid for almost everything, including a beautiful handmade sofa-bed for the main room, lovely large carpets, specially made wood-weave 'curtains' and a new washing machine. In Canberra he helped me pack and clean on moving day, then travelled with the removalists in their truck, stopping at Graeme's flat in Sydney to pick up the computer desk and chair I'd lent him. When we eventually met up in Barraba, I was shocked to learn that Richard and the burly men with him had failed to collect my things. Graeme and his two flatmates had refused to give them back.

My 700-kilometre drive to Barraba was memorable. It was pouring with rain on the morning of the move, and it continued all day. I'd had some very busy days packing and preparing. The removalists had arrived earlier than expected, before I'd completed the packing. I was doing the final cleaning myself, and the men's wet and muddy boots added to my difficulties in leaving everything spotless. A friend had advised me to take a back route—one I'd not travelled on before. When I reached the motorway I discovered I

MANY MOVES AND MUCH ACTIVITY

was on a one-way road heading towards Melbourne! If only we'd had smartphones and satellite navigation then! Visibility was so bad that drivers of cars on the motorway had to pull over and stop, then crawl along, eyes straining and probably with fingers crossed. Large sticks and tree branches were strewn all along the road. And here I was travelling south, when my destination was way up north. I felt pretty inadequate and somewhat nervous. I eventually reached a tiny service station and asked for directions to get to the road I needed. I was soaking wet by the time I got to the counter and sought help. I've never been one to eat sweets/lollies when travelling, but I went back to the car with a block of chocolate and fed myself a piece at regular intervals. I'd packed grapes and cheese for my lunch, and I stopped at a cafe for an evening meal. By the time I arrived in Barraba I was feeling quite comfortable. We all slept that night at Andy's Backpackers (now Andy's Guesthouse) and the moving in and unpacking took place the next morning.

All was well. Richard returned to England. I bought lots of fruit trees and planted them in my backyard. I planted an apricot and a cherry tree in the front, and I prepared and planted beds of vegetables and herbs. Of course, at Andy's request, I agreed to start up a LETSystem. Andy had been a member of the Blue Mountains system when I was in Katoomba, and he'd spoken to the mayor about me and about LETS. She invited me to address the next council meeting.

It wasn't long before we were up and running. A LETS member with expertise in landscaping designed for me the most attractive front yard and driveway. Friends helped build a carport, a brick patio in front of the house and a pergola along the back—which I planted with grapevines. Curved beds of flowers, shrubs and attractive foliage replaced the former grass lawn in the front. The house had the best view, looking out at a level crossing over the Manilla River, with hills behind. I loved watching the sun and moon rising over those hills and being reflected in the water.

It seems that anyone who's lived in Barraba describes it as 'a special place'. I certainly found it to be so. The people were most welcoming. For a tiny, isolated town it offered a lot, and I soon got involved in many activities. I joined Barrapella, an a capella choir. I joined the Anglican church choir, and later became the church's organist. I joined a Tai Chi class, and I even joined the Barraba Shire Brass Band and played in it for the ten years I was there. I was offered an instrument and free lessons, so I began with the cornet before moving on to the tenor horn, which was easier for me to blow.

Soon after I moved to Barraba, Wendy and Paul separated. She had told him to leave, and he had; and he'd quickly started a new relationship. Wendy came over for a lengthy visit with her daughter, Eden, then about six months old. She was planning to divorce Paul. She was hurting and angry at him but, despite that, she and Eden had a lovely time in Barraba. They met all of my friends, visited farms, rode horses, and Wendy was out socialising most evenings while I babysat. One of the young mothers Wendy met said she wanted her daughter to have piano lessons.

MANY MOVES AND MUCH ACTIVITY

'My Mum will teach her', said Wendy. And so it was that I returned to teaching piano.

And I loved it. My pupils came to my home for their weekly lessons, and I was most happy to be spending lots of one-on-one time with children again. Later, I voluntarily started a choir at the high school, and organised and assisted at professional brass lessons for primary children at both the Catholic and state schools. An experienced Tamworth Conservatorium teacher travelled the 100 kilometres each way to take these classes.

Singing in Barrapella was another great joy. This choir was once described as 'a drinking group with a singing problem'. Once a week we met at Andy's in the early evening. Some of the choir members came straight from work, so our host (and leading bass singer) always had chilled beer, wine, crackers and dips at the ready. In wintertime there was a welcoming log fire. Our lovely and most capable choir director was not a pianist, so all the singing was unaccompanied. We sang a huge variety of songs from many countries and in many languages, and our vast repertoire included a number of gospel songs. At performances, everything was sung from memory. There were some fabulous voices there.

When that initial musical director left the area, the choir paid for school music teachers to travel from Tamworth and from Bingara to lead the choir. Eventually they too moved, and I went from singing 'tenor' to standing out front and being the musical director. By that time, we were singing a few accompanied songs, so I sometimes directed from the piano. Barrapella always entered the

JUST AN ORDINARY PERSON

Gunnedah eisteddfod and was often invited to sing away from home. Two memorable choir events under my leadership were at the town of Bingara, some sixty-two kilometres away.

The first was a concert put on to celebrate the restoration and reopening of the magnificent Roxy Theatre—a former Art Deco movie theatre that had been closed for forty years before being beautifully and lovingly transformed into a multipurpose cinema and regional centre for the performing arts. Bob Carr, the then-Premier of NSW, was a special guest, and we performed our show piece 'Oh Happy Day' (the *Sister Act* version).

The second Bingara event was in that same hall, but it was a dramatic stage production based on Dickens' *A Christmas Carol*. I'd been asked to select and train a small group of choristers to play the roles of English carol singers. We were required to sing a number of traditional carols, some onstage and some offstage, throughout the many performances. We also sang a bracket of carols in the foyer as the audiences arrived. I'll never forget how hot and uncomfortable it was backstage, in the dark, in the middle of that hot summer. We were dressed in thick, floor-length, long-sleeved, high-necked costumes and had to hold torches on our scripts as we strained to hear our cues.

As a member of the Barraba band, I had equally enjoyable and interesting experiences. We were a very happy group—relaxed, but playing well. We rehearsed every Thursday night, and we performed at just about every function held in Barraba, as well as in processions, street parades and sometimes concerts in other towns.

MANY MOVES AND MUCH ACTIVITY

I have the strongest memories of the day we led the parade at the Tamworth Country Music Festival. Immediately in front of us were police horses, dropping manure just ahead of our feet as we endeavoured to keep in a straight line behind the band member ahead of us as we marched three abreast, using our peripheral vision to keep in line with those on either side—all while reading and playing from the tiny sheet of music attached to our instruments. It was reminiscent of Irish dancing—from waist up we were fairly static, but our feet were going in all directions as we tried not to step in the fresh manure.

In Barraba I was also a member of a Sai Baba group. Carol, who'd run my spiritual healing workshop at Findhorn, had been a Sai Baba devotee, and since hearing about him from her in 1986 I'd felt the presence of this guru whenever I prepared to give healing to others. Sathya Sai Baba (1926 - 2011) was an Indian spiritual leader with followers in some 126 countries. Hinduism was his religion, but he urged his devotees to adhere to their own religions, be the best they could be and live a life of service to others. 'Love all. Serve all. Help ever. Hurt never'. was how he summed up his philosophy. Sai Baba himself established free hospitals, clinics, schools and drinking water, among other helpful projects.

My friend Judy was a devotee, and had been attending regular Sai Baba gatherings for devotional singing and prayers before she moved to Barraba. Several of her Sai Baba friends had also relocated there, so they formed a local group and I joined them. It was helpful that I was an active member of the local Anglican church, as some people regarded us as members of a rival religion. In fact there was a day when the Church of England minister visited me in my home, sat down, and very seriously told me that I was 'keeping bad company'. He believed my friends had led me astray. And I was in my mid sixties! I felt I was back in 12th-century France at the time of the Inquisition.

CHAPTER 14

RELATIONSHIPS NEW AND OLD

I'd not been in Barraba long when I met JL. He was always referred to by his first two initials, though I came to call him Johnny. I was sixty-one and he was eighty-one when we met. JL was a widower who lived alone. He'd been a farmer, and he'd also worked nights as caretaker at the nearby asbestos factory (now closed) when times were tough.

A slim, energetic man, always smartly dressed and well groomed, he had a sharp wit and an honesty that could, at times, be shocking. I was with him once in the main street of Barraba when he met up with a woman he'd not seen for some time. His opening remark was, 'Blimey! You've put on some weight!' JL always said what was on his mind.

I'd never known anyone like him. Here was a man still living in the house he was born in—a true Aussie 'man of the land' who called women 'sheilas', and whose vocabulary included many Australian colloquialisms and slang. But he'd been educated at a top private school, loved classical music (especially opera), was forever quoting Shakespeare, had a keen interest in everything and was knowledgable in many subjects.

JL had a fine singing voice and since he was seven years old had sung in the church choir, which I'd joined. This lively old man also had a reputation for being a flirt—a ladies' man. He'd always enjoyed the company of women, though come Anzac Day he was very much a man's man, as he enjoyed his beer and played two-up at the local RSL. JL had served overseas in World War II, and wore his medals with pride.

He was a gentleman of the 'old school'. He liked to open the car door for a woman. He was caring and considerate. His attentions to me led to us becoming more than good company. I fell in love with him, and our relationship became an intimate one. It was a lovely time for both of us, as he got to know and spend time with my friends and I met all of his family and friends. We watched the Wimbledon tennis matches together until 3 am. We danced together for hours at a fancy dress ball. I held parties at his house. At one time I bought an organ at a sale and, because of its size, it resided in his enormous living room.

When I told Richard, in a letter, that I was in love with someone, he said nothing, but it was a blow to him and his hopes of us reuniting. Soon afterwards he began a relationship himself, even becoming engaged, but it was short-lived. In the time leading up to

RELATIONSHIPS NEW AND OLD

Richard's next Christmas visit to Barraba, I was wondering how he and JL would get on together. JL had previously turned up at my door whenever an unmarried man had visited me—as if staking his territory. I remember the day a male friend arrived with a small metal shovel he'd made for my fireplace. JL drove up and strode down the path to my front door, looking tall and commanding—and he wasn't a tall man. He walked in, politely shook hands with my friend, and stayed until the man left.

But when Richard arrived, he and JL were like old friends reuniting after a long absence. It was an extremely hot day, and we all went to JL's place for a swim in his pool. Graeme was with us, as he was now living with me in Barraba. As the four of us relaxed and cooled off in the water, JL burst into song—one of his favourite hymns. Richard, Graeme and I joined in, adding harmony parts. We continued singing some familiar hymns together in the pool. It was wonderful, though it would have seemed most odd to any bystander. After a while we decided to go inside so I could accompany the voices on the organ. With the aid of some hymn books, the four of us allocated the soprano, alto, tenor and bass parts between us. All three men had the ability to sing any part well. With the organ enriching the sound, we worked our way through the hymn book. It was extraordinary. I'd believed in reincarnation for some thirty years. I now felt convinced that this wasn't the first time we four had sung sacred music together.

On 29 February, in the leap year of 2000, I handed JL a typewritten 'marriage proposal'. I really wanted to be married to him and share his life fully.

JUST AN ORDINARY PERSON

'What a waste of paper', he replied. It hurt. But at least I knew where I stood. He told me that for him, marriage was for life, even if one of the couple had already died. (His daughter did mention to me later, though, that they'd talked about his marrying me, but she considered I was 'too strong a person'.) Anyway, as time went on, I was pleased that my proposal wasn't accepted. It's very strange, but one tiny incident changed my feelings completely, and from then on we were just good friends. JL came to my front door one morning and I greeted him with a kiss before he came inside, and I was hit by the smell of BO from his sports jacket! Tony's jumper had been the trigger for my feelings for him back in 1956, and now, nearly fifty years later, a sports coat was switching similar feelings off.

We remained the best of friends for JL's remaining years, and spent much of our time together. He was helping me in the garden one day when he slipped on a wet wooden stepping stone while carrying buckets of water in each hand. He broke his leg, was hospitalised in Tamworth and developed pneumonia. His family came from far and wide and, fortunately, a son and daughter were with him and playing his favourite operatic music when he died. My last visit was the night before, when we spent a really lovely couple of hours together.

* * *

By the time of my move to Barraba, Graeme had spent all of his share of the money from the Katoomba house sale. He'd met up with a man, Chris, at one of Sydney's games arcades, and had been persuaded to move in with him and another young man who were sharing a flat close to the city. Graeme could never say no to Chris, though for some months he was able to say no to trying the marijuana that Chris and his friend regularly offered to share with him.

At school in Katoomba, in his mid-teens, Graeme had taken to heart the information his class was given about illegal drugs. Afterwards, he had come home and talked to me about it. 'Mummy, I'm never going to take drugs', he said. And he meant it.

When living in Sydney with Chris, Graeme, now twenty, was drinking beer, smoking cigarettes and engaging in minor criminal activities such as stealing milk money. But he drew the line at illegal substances—until, at a party one night where everyone else was happily sharing cannabis, Chris told him, 'Have a few beers first, Gra, then you'll like it'. Graeme did as suggested, and became addicted.

I'd only been in Barraba a couple of weeks when I was woken at three in the morning by a phone call from a policeman in Sydney's Kings Cross. He'd found Graeme wandering around, unable to say who he was or where he lived. My phone number was in his wallet. The policeman said to me, 'I thought he was worth helping. Can you come now and get your son?'

I immediately drove the 500 kilometres, picked up Graeme and drove to his flat. The other two roommates had left. A sign on the door indicated that all three had been evicted due to arrears in rent. I decided to collect what I could of Graeme's belongings, and take him and his possessions back to Barraba. Graeme was in no state to say or do anything, but he did walk into his flat with me.

The smell and the filth of the place was overwhelming. I found wet sheets in the washing machine that had been there for weeks. They were slimy and stank. Half-eaten food and dirty pots and pans were on the floor. I packed up my car and, with Graeme half asleep in the back seat, I did the six-hour trip back home.

At first, Graeme lived with me. Once he'd recovered from this psychotic episode and was able to tell me about his difficulties, we talked together about the best course of action to take. Evidently Chris had run up enormous debts. Using Graeme's computer and data, he'd actually courted and 'married' a woman in America! Everything was in Graeme's name. So, apart from his personal problems, Graeme had telcos and other companies—as well as the landlord—demanding payments. Graeme was now on a disability pension, with no way of repaying the debts. I sought information on bankruptcy; it seemed to be the only option. So Graeme declared himself bankrupt. His watch was the only thing of any value he owned. (If memory serves me right, he was allowed to keep it.) His debts were all 'wiped'. He could now start again with a clean slate.

Through the local doctor and hospital I arranged for Graeme's medical treatment. A nurse would visit us regularly to give an injection. I drove him to Tamworth for a number of one-hour counselling sessions with a psychologist. We looked into possible rehabilitation programs.

RELATIONSHIPS NEW AND OLD

Graeme went on to spend ten years in Barraba, on and off. Being an excellent trombone player, he was quickly snapped up and warmly welcomed as a member of the band. He was probably at his happiest there. They were such a loving and caring group of people, and the music making was an enriching experience. Graeme also joined and enjoyed singing with the Barrapella choir, and even sang a solo part when the choir made a recording. He also performed in an Old Time Music Hall event, and played piano solos in several concerts I put on. He played the piano in a way that touched people, taking his listeners to another place.

However, Graeme's addictions to drugs and gambling still sabotaged his life and created great difficulties in my relationship with him. I was trying everything I could to help him. It's heartbreaking to see someone you love 'messing up their life'. Under the influence of drugs, Graeme's behaviour was psychotic. He truly was like a Jekyll and Hyde. In fact, he was officially diagnosed as schizophrenic, though one doctor told me that his mental problems were all drug-related.

Graeme had a number of run-ins with the police while in the Barraba area. I remember attending his court hearings in Manila and in Tamworth. And he was in and out of several mental hospitals and on enforced medication for close to twenty years in all. He had three visits to rehabilitation centres, but always left before the programs were completed. I can't recall the number of professional people he saw, to no avail, in an attempt to free himself of his addictions to drugs and gambling.

JUST AN ORDINARY PERSON

Graeme really wanted to make something of his life. He had the ability to be accepted at three universities without the usual qualifications. His auditions and applications for places in numerous TAFE courses were always successful. At Armidale University he did two years of a course for music teaching in schools. His composition teacher there had a very high regard for his work and ability, and Graeme played the grand piano for the university's formal dinners.

He lived in college at Armidale, and had a girlfriend for most of the time. I met her on a visit to an open day. They planned to marry, and talked about the children they looked forward to having. But after one of his periods in the Armidale mental hospital, she told Graeme that unless he gave up the marijuana, she was ending the relationship. Graeme was heartbroken, and some twenty years later still wondered if he'd be able to track her down and be with her again.

After Armidale, Graeme returned to Barraba. The next tertiary music course he began was in Lismore, then there was one in Western Sydney, then at the University of NSW. The grass was always greener elsewhere.

Graeme's departure from Barraba was as dramatic as his arrival. He had been living with me again, and I'd decided that he had to move out. While I was in my backyard watering the garden one day, Graeme just got into my car and drove it to Sydney! I'd heard nothing. But Graeme, his possessions and my car had gone. I contacted the police, and eventually the car was found in Sydney. I did the eight-hour trip by coach and train to pick it up. At the time I'd been working through the book *A Course in Miracles* (I'd first read it when it came out in 1976), and I was regarding my challenges as opportunities, and seeing Graeme my greatest teacher. I didn't say that to him, of course, but I was able to deal with everything 'philosophically', and I always expected the best.

Richard didn't share my viewpoint and optimism. He'd been disappointed after the failure of early efforts to help, having given Graeme emotional and financial support several times. He no longer held out hopes for his rehabilitation. Richard didn't want to be disappointed and hurt again.

Graeme settled once more in Sydney. At first he moved in with his older brother, Martin. But after stealing and selling Martin's large collection of CDs, Martin insisted on Graeme moving out and had the locks changed. Graeme then went into privately rented accommodation, which he lost (along with all his possessions) while doing a residential rehab program in Wagga Wagga. He then managed to get a government housing flat at Glebe, in Sydney. Dressed as a girl, he gave his story to a newspaper journalist who did an article about him (as Sarah) with a photo taken in his empty apartment. As a result, he was inundated with goods—a fridge, microwave, TV, a bed, furniture and clothing. But it was as Graeme that he had a studio photograph taken, acted as an extra in the film *Babe: Pig in the City*, had singing lessons and sang at a few weddings. He also joined the Sydney University choir, though he was not a student there, attended a choir camp and sang in some of their concerts.

JUST AN ORDINARY PERSON

***

Simon had completed his Advanced Science degree at the end of 1994, and decided to use the money from the Katoomba house sale to support himself for a year of further private study before enrolling for a Ph.D. During that year of study he also did some university tutoring, and took dance classes with some of his university friends at the Fred Astaire Dance Studios in Sydney. After six months of lessons, he was invited to undergo training as a dance teacher. Simon never did get back to university. He taught dance at the Fred Astaire studios from 1996 to 1999. The pay was low, but while there he taught Cate Blanchett and Andrew Upton the dance for their wedding; and while teaching dance he met the girl he would later marry—the loveliest daughter-in-law I could ever wish for.

While Simon was managing on a shoestring, his university colleagues were enjoying highly paid jobs in the IT sector. After three years at the dance studio, he applied for a job as an analyst/programmer, had an interview, and was offered the job. And he continued to do IT work, sometimes on a contract basis, until he retired.

In 2002 Simon read the book *How to Develop a Perfect Memory* and was fascinated by it. In early 2003 he heard about the Australian Memory Championships, held in Melbourne each August, and decided to enter. There were many events—memorising random words, numbers, decks of card, names and faces, etc. Simon trained for just six months and, to the surprise of the other

RELATIONSHIPS NEW AND OLD

'regular' competitors, he won the championship. In fact, he entered and won it another three times; and he did well in the World Championship in 2005. I went to Melbourne with him for one of them, getting the train from Barraba then flying from Sydney. I found it interesting and enjoyable—though I must admit my heart was in my mouth as I watched him compete in the live events. Simon's interest in memory training has continued and he has created software for overseas memory competitions, and continues to work with American colleagues in memory training and competition platforms.

* * *

While living in Barraba, I did some quite unexpected paid 'caring' work. It all started when a neighbour was cut off by floodwater and couldn't get back to town after a day in Tamworth. She was a nurse, and did part-time overnight caring at a house quite close to our street. She phoned me and asked if I could take her place that night. I was to provide my own bedding and pillow, and be there from 8 pm to 8 am. I agreed to help, collected my things and went to the address. I introduced myself to Mrs G, who told me where to find the fold-up bed I was to set up outside her bedroom door. I would sleep there, but be available if she needed anything overnight. At 6 am sharp I was to feed the cat, after having dressed and put my bed away. At 6:15 I was to take her a cup of tea. I was then to cut up the dog's raw meat and take it outside to its large walk-in kennel. I was to use a shovel to collect the dog poo, then hose the concrete floor. I was then to prepare Mrs G's breakfast, and it had to be 'just so'. Obviously I did well enough, as I was asked to join the list of regular carers. She had someone there 24/7, with three, four-hour shifts during the day, as well as the overnight one, all organised by her solicitor.

Mrs G had lived a very active life on a farming property well out of town. Her husband had died many years before; they had no children. Eventually, her severe arthritis forced her to move into town, which she hated. Having little control over her physical activities, she took what control she could when dealing with her carers. She was very fussy about her food. On one occasion, as soon as she'd tasted the meal I'd prepared, she demanded I wrap it in newspaper and throw it into the bin. And I'd followed her instructions exactly in preparing it.

I soon discovered that anything I admired in her place 'disappeared' as soon as I left that day. She was full of fear; she thought I might steal it. Never was any carer permitted to be alone in her house. If we were on duty and she was taken away briefly for chiropody or a haircut, we had to leave and the place was locked—even the gate was padlocked. We'd be phoned when it was time to return.

Mrs G died less than twenty-four hours after my last overnight stay. Surprisingly, the last breakfast I cooked and served her brought her first compliment.

'I've never had poached eggs cooked so well', she said. Her approval meant a lot to me. It was a great way to end our time together.

RELATIONSHIPS NEW AND OLD

After that, I was asked to stay overnight with other elderly and infirm women who lived alone, and I was very happy to be able to help them. With one of them I had a very special relationship, and was treated like family. Even though I was almost seventy and she in her eighties, I felt as if she was my grandmother, and loved the time spent with her. She could no longer get out and about, and enjoyed hearing of all the things I was doing. On two occasions I was with her overnight on New Year's Eve. Both times I took my small TV and set it up in her bedroom before she went to sleep. I'd wake her at about 11:50 pm and together we'd watch the midnight fireworks in Sydney Harbour.

Work of a very different nature was chairing the Clifton Hall Restoration Project. Barraba had a heritage-listed Art Deco cinema, which had for many years been closed. It was owned by a local man who, with his wife, used the premises to publish the Barraba Gazette newspaper. Their office and the printing presses were in the building. Clifton Hall adjoined Andy's. Some years before I left Barraba, Andy and I, along with several of our friends, formed a committee to look into buying and restoring the beautiful old building and running it as a cinema again. Many towns were doing this, and state government grants were available to assist with the costs. At the time, our nearest cinema was in Tamworth, 100 kilometres away.

Years of work went into the project, which I headed. We visited and communicated with people who'd been successful with similar enterprises. We engaged a heritage listed architect and had plans drawn up and costed, and we surveyed the entire community—I visited door to door. The building's owner had agreed to a selling price. We held a number of fundraising events—variety show, music hall, etc.—to ensure fifty percent of the total cost could be paid by the community. We did all the work required to incorporate the group, produced a detailed business plan and prepared the applications for the necessary grants. The local council members had been kept informed, and some were supportive. But the one thing we needed and didn't get was official council approval. After my final address to a Barraba Council meeting, a short time before its amalgamation under the Tamworth umbrella, we were informed that the council would not be supporting our project. I was later told that Clifton Hall's owner hadn't really wanted to sell and had put a high price on, thinking we wouldn't pay it. He was good friends with some of the councillors.

It was a blow. The money donated had to be returned, and the rest of the money was given to the festival committee. But I was thrilled when a member of our group decided to buy one of the four main street hotels. A local architect worked with him and, after some years, that former pub became The Playhouse Hotel, offering five-star accommodation, a superb venue for meetings and conferences, a cafe with amazing food and a theatre-cum-cinema! Barraba residents can now see a film most weekends, and visitors come from all over the country to events held there or to stay in top-class accommodation while visiting the area. The Playhouse Hotel was still a work in progress when I left, but I've since been back and had the pleasure of staying there.

*　*　*

Quite a lot of my voluntary work in Barraba involved playing the piano/organ and playing in the band. For many years I visited the local retirement home each week and played the piano for community singing for the residents. I accompanied a lovely soprano from the church choir, and everyone joined in as we sang the well-known old songs. It's wonderful that memories of tunes and words remain, even when short-term memory has gone. People who spent their days just sitting in a chair came to life and joined in the singing.

On Sundays I played the organ for the 7:30 am service at the Anglican church. I would go home for breakfast and change out of the black skirt and white blouse with black ribbon bow at my neck, and put on the brass band uniform. Then, with my tenor horn and some very different books of music, I'd play in the band at the Salvation Army morning service. And if the Catholic church organist was away or ill, after a quick lunch I'd play for the Catholic service at 2 pm.

Barraba had (and at the time of writing, still has) an outstanding adult education organisation. It arranges classes of all kinds in other country towns as well as in Barraba. I was a member of its committee during my years there, and enjoyed it very much.

Something quite different, but which had some members in common, was the local wine society. When I arrived in Barraba I was a teetotaler, but when I left I was 'running' its wine society! This group met in one another's homes once a month. Each person brought something to contribute to the three-course (plus nibbles), home-cooked meal. One of the members would bring the wines and talk about them—that's where the organisation came in. To be decided were the dates, the venue, the menu and who would bring what. Everything was arranged by telephone. They were lovely get-togethers. The food, of course, was always superb; country towns have the best cooks. And the relaxed socialising and conversation in beautiful homes was something we all looked forward to from month to month.

***

I left Barraba in January 2006, after a stay of over nine years. Twelve months earlier I'd felt in need of a break, and decided to have a week away at a camping ground suggested by Judy. After cancelling some *thirty commitments*, I drove to Rainbow Beach on the coast and totally relaxed in a one-room cabin. I prepared simple meals for myself, and walked on the adjacent beach every morning and evening. I listened to inspirational tapes, and read an interesting book.

'I could live like this', I thought.

On my return I talked to Judy. I mentioned that I'd never lived close to water, and I felt a strong desire to move to a beach. To my surprise she said, 'I haven't yet told anyone, but I've decided to move to Pearl Beach. I wonder if that's where you'll go'.

RELATIONSHIPS NEW AND OLD

Pearl Beach has been described as the most beautiful beachside village on the Central Coast of New South Wales. Less than forty kilometres north of Sydney, it faces Broken Bay, a large inlet of the Tasman Sea, and is surrounded by national parkland. It has a small population—just 536 in the 2016 census. I had been there once, but hadn't been out of the car. The holiday cottage we went to with Richard each Christmas was on the other side of that bay, and we'd gone for a drive to Patonga one day and had detoured down the hill to Pearl Beach before continuing 'home'.

Judy had stayed there, and knew the area well. It was where her daughter had chosen to be married; the beach and the native arboretum were popular venues for weddings. Judy invited me to spend a weekend in Pearl Beach with her, to see if I might like to live there, too. From the moment I arrived, I knew it would be the perfect place for me. But it was an expensive place. It's where celebrities had weekenders. The weekly rental of a beachfront house, in the season, was sixty-eight times the rent I was paying.

So I made it a project! For the next twelve months I took steps to manifest a move to a lovely, affordable place in Pearl Beach. I had no capital, and only a pension income apart from occasional caring work and playing the organ at funerals. But I'd made up my mind.

I came across two wonderful books by American feng shui expert Stephanie Roberts. One was titled *Fast Feng Shui for Prosperity* and it was full of useful advice and suggested activities for working on oneself and one's environment. I began to clear up my clutter. Over the months I thoroughly went through everything I possessed—every piece of paper in the filing cabinet, every item of clothing, as I progressed room by room. And, most importantly, I started a '108 Desires List'. This is a list of 108 things you want to be, do or have. It can include material goods, activities and experiences, and 'taking care of business' (such as paying off a loan or debt). Using an exercise book or a computer, you build the list, numbering the desires. Each morning, you begin the day by reading them, crossing off the ones you've received or decided you no longer want, then adding new ones—always keeping the total at 108. It was fun, and it worked for me. I'd sit up in bed with my special book first thing each day. I was so enthusiastic about this exercise that I was telling all my friends about it.

I also placed various 'wealth symbols' in each room, along with postcards of Pearl Beach. And I recall putting blue dolphin fridge magnets in the form of PB on my fridge. Each day I wrote in my journal, 'I'm really happy living in Pearl Beach. I'm looking out at beautiful trees. I'm enjoying the sound of the waves'. And I pictured myself living there, and felt gratitude.

Six months later, Judy made her move from Barraba. She rented a house in Pearl Beach initially, and invited me to spend a week there dog-sitting while she holidayed in New Zealand. I jumped at the opportunity, and had a delightful time. I enjoyed long walks with her sweet little dog, I met a number of her neighbours and I spoke to one of her friends who was a semi-retired real estate agent. He didn't think I'd be able to find anything affordable there, but I had a sense that something would work out. I put notes in the letterboxes of two places that were available for rental. One turned out to be a possibility. It was a two-storey house, adapted as two separate residences. The owners used the upstairs rooms for holidays and some weekends, and they were interested in letting the downstairs part to someone who would look after the garden. I met them and was in high hopes. But it wasn't to be. Their son from interstate insisted they keep it free so he could stay there whenever he wanted.

Then Judy rang me with good news. The young man living opposite her place was getting married at the end of the year, and would be moving out of the little 'weekender' he lived in. She'd talked to him and found that several members of his family owned the property, and that one of his uncles dealt with the letting of it. Judy immediately contacted the uncle, and negotiated with him to let me rent the property once it was available. He required that I see it myself before an agreement could be made. So I drove the 450 kilometres, staying with Judy overnight. Of course I was happy to rent this place. I was over the moon! To top it off, Judy had told the uncle of my financial situation, and he offered it to me for less than his nephew was paying. And before I moved in, one of his brothers painted every inch of the interior. It was like going into a brand-new house.

CHAPTER 15

BESIDE THE SEASIDE, BESIDE THE SEA

Richard once said to me, 'I always thought you left England because you needed a break from all that you were doing'. His comment surprised me at the time. I thought it was denial of my decision to leave him. But I now see there was an element of truth in it. In York, in Katoomba and in Barraba, I took on heavy workloads—much of it voluntary work. Looking back now, I suspect that I was unconsciously being driven by my guilt over breaking my marriage vows to Tony, giving up Donna and Gordon, and taking children away from their fathers. I know that in 1982 when I inherited family money after my mother's death, I'd felt unworthy of keeping it. I had the thought that I should use it where it was most needed, and gave a lot away—some of it to strangers. And before leaving England I'd followed the trend of a lot of 'spiritual' people, and got rid of just about all my jewellery and unessential items, telling myself I didn't need 'material things' to be happy.

When I left Barraba and moved to Pearl Beach I was seventy years of age, and I definitely planned to sit back, relax, read books and listen to the waves. However, with Judy living there for six months before I arrived, I was quickly introduced to people who'd been told about me. After just two weeks I was a member of the Pearl Beach Events Committee and was helping to run their many local activities. I stuck to my guns and didn't accept requests to be secretary or chairman of any committees, but I soon found myself very busy indeed. It wasn't until I turned seventy-nine that I took stock and decided to withdraw from all the voluntary local jobs I had taken on. I had a sense that if I didn't, I would be forced to stop, either through illness or accident or death. It seemed very clear to me. But it was difficult for some of the community to accept. I was still there and still able, but no longer 'willing' to be engaged in all I'd been doing. However, my wishes were respected.

My ten years in Pearl Beach were the happiest of times. It certainly is the loveliest place to live, and the community is caring and accepting. I straight away joined the Central Coast LETSystem, and I soon began teaching piano to some children of LETS members (and a couple of adults). Later, word spread and I had some non-LETS pupils. My alternative currency income allowed me to have and do many things I wouldn't have been able to afford using money.

JUST AN ORDINARY PERSON

Not long after I moved to Pearl Beach, there were severe storms and major flooding. Two very tall trees close to the house were loosened. One fell and the other was deemed likely to fall onto the building. The authorities told me I must evacuate until the tree was removed. Fortunately, I was able to stay with Judy until the all clear. But water had come into my house, the bedroom especially. My mattress was wet and musty. A LETS member was offering an almost new innerspring mattress. Another member delivered it to my place and removed the old one. At the time of writing I'm still sleeping soundly on that most comfortable mattress.

Later on, I saw that a local LETS member had recently written a book and was making it available through the system. I immediately contacted her and arranged to collect a copy. My reading of Christine's book, and subsequently meeting with her, led to a close and continuing friendship. I believe LETS is one of the ways many 'old souls' have reconnected this time around.

My first year in Pearl Beach was a census year. In Australia a census is held in August every five years. I'd been a census collector when living in Katoomba and also when in Barraba, so I decided to augment my income and apply again. I was accepted and underwent the training. However, this time things were a little different. Mobile phones were now in use, and instead of having to go home to make landline calls when additional forms were needed, all census collectors were now required to have a mobile phone. So in August 2016 I bought a little Nokia. I've always been interested in new technology and I'm awaiting the day when all our devices and appliances are cord-free. (I've just seen an advertisement for a cordless iron—and I already use a cordless mouse and keyboard and vacuum cleaner—so we're on the way.)

Something I'd never expected to be doing anywhere was running a theatre group, yet that's what I found myself doing a few months after moving to Pearl Beach. Some new residents had arrived; he was a writer, and she had theatrical experience. Her conversations with other parents at the bus stop while waiting to collect their children led to her starting up the Bus Stop Theatre Craft group. Some adults joined, as well as a number of children, and they met weekly to learn theatre skills and to work towards a performance. The members contributed ideas for the storyline and handled the fundraising, promotion and ticket sales. Unfortunately, the planned performance was postponed, and the family then made the decision to move away from the area. The script had not been completed, so the whole production was aborted.

I'd offered my services to help with the music, and had been going along to all the sessions. I felt sorry for the members, left in the lurch. Initially I got them together to do some items in the annual Christmas Carols outdoor event, but then at a party with friends, our host told me how he'd always hoped someone would put on a particular children's musical in Pearl Beach. He was a retired headmaster whose music staff had produced this work. He loved it, and thought it would be ideal to do it locally. So I offered to run with it.

JUST AN ORDINARY PERSON

Pearl Beach is full of amazing people. At that party there were so many wonderful people who were happy to share their skills. One offered to be wardrobe mistress; she'd been a professional dressmaker. A couple with expertise in fashion and design offered to design the costumes. A retired events organiser said she'd do all the publicity, promotion, ticket sales and front-of-house. An artist and set designer was keen to design and paint all the scenery, and the local 'sound and lighting' man wanted to be involved.

It wasn't long before I'd managed to track down and purchase the only existing copy of the work, and gathered together the people to perform it. The Juvenile Operetta *Little Gypsy Gay* (which our members insisted on changing to *Little Gypsy Gaye*) called for a cast of ten children and five adults. It contained some attractive and catchy songs, and had an interesting story about a group of gypsies who found a baby and brought it up as their own. I played the piano accompaniments to the songs, which were interspersed with the script. Two women friends of mine, together with the sound and lighting man, played the adult gypsies. Two tall older children played the baby's parents. It just so happened that the father of one of the cast had built scenery for the Sydney Opera House, so he and I worked with the set designer/painter to produce a very professional set. Rehearsals were held in the Pearl Beach Memorial Hall each Sunday afternoon.

We planned to put on two performances, but ended up doing three shows to packed houses. The children organised and manned a 'gypsy marketplace', which they set up outside the front of the hall after each performance. Here they sold gypsy-type artefacts and food and there was, of course, a gypsy fortune teller. In all, after costs, we were able to donate $2,000 to the Central Coast's autistic school, the choice of our members. A good time was had by all. It goes without saying that the costumes and light and sound effects were as magnificent as the set and scenery.

Our group became the Pearl Beach Youth Theatre group, and I ran it for many years with the support of the parents and a local committee. We put on further musicals, and later performed a melodrama each year as part of the Glee Club Concerts.

Back in the early 1950s, there had been Glee Club Concerts in Pearl Beach and our first one was held to commemorate those. I was, at that time, singing with some Pearl Beach people in a choir that rehearsed in Umina, over the hill. Some of the songs we'd learned there were most suitable, so I arranged to borrow copies of the music and invited some of the choir to sing items in our first concert. Eventually that small group expanded and became known as the Glee Club Choir. We met every week during school terms, and had tremendous fun together. I sometimes referred to us as 'the choir of old crocks', as many of our members were in their eighties—one over ninety—and at times they needed to use walking frames and sticks, even 'headlamps' for one to read the music.

I never began a choir practice without a selection of warm-ups. These were enjoyable but effective ways of limbering up, breathing and generally preparing for singing. I always included humming, tongue twisters, stretching exercises (like picking apples from high up in a tree) and 'blowing raspberries' as we went up and down the scale. We would then sing in four-part harmony as we learned a variety of choral pieces. I generally directed from the piano and accompanied the singers in performances. In the concerts, choir members also took part in many of the non-singing items—some melodramas, skits and comedy routines. I directed and organised five of these annual performances. After I withdrew I was most happy that two of our singers took over, and a further five years of Glee Club Concerts provided great entertainment for locals and visitors. Community singing and audience involvement was always a part of these happy events. I was very surprised and most moved when my community work was acknowledged by a nomination for Australian of the Year in 2011, and by the local council's award for community building in 2012.

***

During my years in Pearl Beach, Graeme was living in Sydney and could easily visit me by train and bus (or on foot from Woy Woy if there were no buses). He spent a lot of time in Pearl Beach and loved being there. He sometimes joined in walks with the Plodders group I belonged to. He sang with the choir, coming to Pearl Beach most Fridays for choir practice. He sometimes acted in the melodramas, and he played piano solos in all but one of the concerts I put on. Unfortunately, for that one, he was on the program and arrived, but was in no state to perform.

The attempts at rehab had not worked. The many appointments with counsellors had come to nothing, as Graeme usually decided not to attend after the first visits. There were times when he arrived at Pearl Beach in such a psychotic state that I felt the need to call the police, and he was taken to a mental hospital for treatment.

One such time he spent some weeks in Wyong hospital, and I visited frequently. The social worker there suggested I handle Graeme's finances in order to ensure his essential bills were paid. We'd previously arranged for his rent to be paid directly from his pension. So after he left hospital (where, incidentally, he was able to buy marijuana from 'over the fence') we went together to a bank and opened a joint account. I had online access to it, and he had a bankcard. This meant I could withdraw his pension money online as soon as it came into his account and use it to pay his bills. And I must admit that on a Thursday night I would withdraw it all, to ensure he came to Pearl Beach for the Friday rehearsals. I always provided him with plenty of pensioner train tickets so he could travel. Once he arrived, I would give him his money, and I would often then drive him to Umina so he could buy tobacco, papers and filters to make his cigarettes. Looking back, this kind of interference in the desire to be helpful is not one I'd recommend. Graeme may have enjoyed his singing, acting and playing piano in Pearl Beach, but it definitely disempowered him in another way. Even though there was a Tribunal hearing during a time of hospitalisation in Sydney, and the NSW Trustee & Guardian were given control of Graeme's money, his 'pocket money' continued to be paid into the joint account. This still enabled me to exercise control. There were so many times Graeme and I had agreed to me transferring a certain sum—but he would get to an ATM by 6:18 pm (the moment the money was in the account) and draw out all but the odd cents. There were times we were playing 'cat and mouse'. He was at an ATM in Sydney; I was at home on my phone, watching for the moment the money appeared in his account. I would set an alarm earlier in the day. Sometimes I got there first, other times he did. It didn't make for an ideal relationship, even though it was with Graeme's prior approval that I made the transfers, as a rule. Graeme rarely had the use of a phone, and making contact with him was usually impossible. If it was essential for me to contact him, the only way was to transfer all the money as soon as it went into his account. He'd then find a way of phoning me immediately. (I used to regret the demise of the old telegram, where urgent messages were delivered to the door.)

It had not been possible to get a landline phone connected in his flat, and Graeme would hock any mobile phone as soon as he had one. In fact, anything of any value was hocked and not redeemed. Books and music I'd given him, TV sets, hi-fi equipment, piano keyboards and a new trombone were all taken to various pawn shops. Graeme always had the intention of getting them out again, and there were times I helped him do that, transferring his money to my account and paying at the shop. I remember occasions when, together, we struggled as we carried large and heavy equipment on the bus and the several-block walk from the bus stop to his flat. But we might as well have saved our energy. The next pay day, Graeme would be out of money again, and he'd somehow manage to get the stuff back to the shop. It was all lost in the end.

BESIDE THE SEASIDE, BESIDE THE SEA

The Trustee & Guardian arranged for 'food vouchers' to ensure he had money for food. But Graeme would use the card to buy tobacco and soft drinks, then go straight to his local tobacconist who would take the goods for fifty percent of their cost. This man would also 'mind' any mobile phone, giving $5 for it. I felt like speaking to the guy or reporting him, but Graeme said there were plenty of others doing the same.

After paying for drugs (which now included 'ice'), smokes, coffee, sugar and toilet paper, any money Graeme had went straight into the nearest poker machine. It was rare for him to have anything left half an hour after withdrawing all his money. His pension was being deposited into his account twice a week instead of fortnightly, but that only meant he used drugs twice a week and gambled twice a week. The rest of his time was usually spent sleeping or having coffee and cigarettes with neighbours in a similar situation to his. Graeme's clothes were only washed when he visited me, as it cost $2 to use the machine at his place. His only haircuts over a period of twenty-plus years were when he was with me, and I arranged the payment.

During my ten years in Pearl Beach we often discussed living together as a way of helping Graeme with his many problems. In fact, I once made application to rent a most beautiful home in Koolewong for Graeme, Martin and me to share. I was bitterly disappointed when it fell through after difficulties with Graeme's application, which the Trustee & Guardian failed to prepare properly. But I now realise that it would not have been best for any of us.

JUST AN ORDINARY PERSON

My home in Pearl Beach was a small cabin with a large deck, a shed and an outside toilet. I was later to learn that officially there wasn't even a shed on that land. When Graeme stayed with me, he either slept on the sofa bed in the main room, or on a large hammock on the deck outside. He would always arrive hungry and ready to sleep. He slept most of the time. In wet weather he needed to be inside, and I had piano pupils from time to time. So I bought a tent through LETS and had it erected behind the house. Friends provided a fold-up bed. The agreed plan was for Graeme to stay with me full-time for a period of rehabilitation. He would not gamble or buy any illegal drugs. For five months he slept in the tent, but kept finding reasons for 'quick trips' back to Sydney. I would accompany him, but it didn't work as we'd hoped—though he did get to do quite a bit of musical composition while at my place.

Graeme composed some beautiful music; it spoke directly to the heart. One of his songs was called 'Sister', and he wrote it in honour of his sister Jennifer. Graeme was just four years old when she died. He was very sensitive and felt deeply about things. When Simon married in 2007, Graeme wrote a piece for the occasion, and sat at a grand piano and played it as guests arrived for the reception. And he wrote music to be played for my funeral, and even for Simon's funeral.

We generally enjoyed our time together. When he wasn't sleeping, we talked a lot and usually played Scrabble or Upwords at mealtimes. He called me 'the Queen of Upwords', though we were on a par, generally, at word games. We also enjoyed regular music-making. I accompanied him in the Italian arias he loved to sing. We played piano duets. I'd help him learn the choir music when he'd missed rehearsals, and we worked together as we prepared choral music for the annual Armidale choral weekend each March. I'd been to seventeen of them, and he'd been with me for ten.

* * *

A few months after I arrived in Pearl Beach I had the idea of writing some simple verses based on what I considered to be the essential truths of all religions and spiritual practices. It seemed to me that the organised religions had lost the plot to some extent, and were no longer reaching the majority of people. My intention was to write for children. I'd grown up with *A Child's Garden of Verse,* and my working title for my book was *A Child's Heaven of Verse.* I wrote twenty-two rhythmic, rhyming verses and then signed up with an online literary agent with a view to having them published. (Self-publishing wasn't an easy option then.) It was months before I discovered that this 'agency' was a scam. I managed to get out of the contract, but my enthusiasm had gone. I emailed my book to a couple of publishers, but heard nothing. I had the thought of adding illustrations, and discussed it with one of the youth theatre members who was a talented artist. I think he was ten when he drew coloured pictures for each of the verses—based on my concepts. A friend then assisted me with preparing those illustrations for adding to the text on computer. I also considered having an accompanying CD. Graeme generously set all the verses to music, and we did a rough recording on my iPad of him singing and accompanying himself on the piano. I even gave a short author talk about this 'book' at a local writer's event, and was pleased with the reception. But despite everyone's efforts, the project stalled. I now intend to self-publish those verses after completing this memoir.

I did have a little literary success, however. My friend Christine had a short story selected for the first volume of *Seniors' Stories,* organised by NSW Seniors Card; and the following year, when they again invited online submissions, I decided to enter. I sent off a short story, which was one of 100 accepted for the book from 1,000 entries. And I was one of eleven people invited to read their story onstage in the City Recital Hall during Seniors' Week.

* * *

By 2011 Graeme's mental health problems and behaviour prevented him from taking part in many family activities. Years earlier, he and his friends had broken into Simon's flat and stolen his valuable violin along with other items; and Simon had been threatened by people coming to his home demanding he pay them money owed by his brother. The last straw came after Simon and his wife moved to a new house with their first baby. They were disturbed and violently threatened at 6 o'clock one morning by Graeme's 'best friend'. Soon after this, their house was burgled, the back window smashed to gain entry. Simon believed that Graeme was responsible (though Graeme assured me he was not involved). But Simon decided that, for the sake of his family, he had no alternative to cutting off all contact with Graeme.

BESIDE THE SEASIDE, BESIDE THE SEA

It was distressing for all concerned. Graeme had been at the hospital with me the day Simon's first baby was born, and he had great love for them all. But he accepted it. In the years that followed, Martin and Graeme would visit me on Christmas Day, and the three of us would celebrate together. On a different day (or different time of day) Martin and I would have the Christmas meal with Simon and his family. I feel so sad as I write this. Family meant a lot to Graeme. But the last time he'd attended a full family gathering, he'd arrived completely stoned at the expensive restaurant Richard had booked for us all. It was most uncomfortable and embarrassing for everyone.

I understood it from Graeme's point of view. He was so disappointed in himself and his life choices. Time after time he'd enthusiastically begun new courses of study, only to drop out after a short while. His efforts to find employment followed a similar pattern. He would get a job in a call centre, but stop going after a few weeks. Having to front up to his father on his arrival each December and admit to failure, yet again, became too painful for him. Marijuana always made him feel good, so he'd use that just before meeting Richard each year, but with dire consequences.

I always had the hope and expectation that Graeme would change. I probably needed to believe that in order to accept the frequent verbal abuse, occasional physical threats and the many disappointments. Graeme rarely turned up for medical or dental appointments. There were several times he didn't turn up for a concert performance. I remember one choir concert at Barraba when he was to be the only tenor, and he didn't show up at all. There was no such thing as a mobile phone. I had to wait until the end of the concert before driving to his home to investigate, and help him get treatment. I never knew from one day to the next which personality state Graeme would be in.

To add to the complications, Graeme had major 'gender issues'. When living in Barraba he always dressed as a man in public, but in his bedroom at my place, and in the homes he rented, he liked to dress as a woman. He'd discussed his desire to live as a woman with the first psychologist I took him to. The sessions had been recorded on cassette tape, and Richard and I both listened to them with Graeme, afterwards. At that time, Graeme accepted the counsellor's opinion that trans-gendering was not the answer, and that it would be far better for him to continue as Graeme. But in Sydney, his GP would always give him a prescription for oestrogen. He took advantage of that, and whenever he had no money for 'feel-good' illegal substances he would visit her for the legal ones.

My own thoughts were that he was unhappy with his life as a man, and the idea of stepping aside from it all and beginning again as a different person was incredibly appealing. Graeme had told me in Katoomba of his first sexual experience with a girl who had physically hurt him. Though he was only attracted to women, and expected to marry and have children, he didn't seem to be comfortable as an adult male.

From time to time Graeme seriously planned to live permanently as a woman. He began having regular counselling at Sydney's Gender Centre. As part of the program there, he did a drawing of two people. Using coloured pencils, he depicted himself two ways—on the left, as a tense and troubled man and, on the right, as an attractive, contented woman. They were labelled 'Graeme, unhappy man' and 'Gia, happy transsexual woman'.

In November 2013, Graeme and I travelled to Uluru, the 'red heart' of Australia. On this occasion I was most grateful for his support and his talents, though when he arrived at my place the evening before our flight, he was thoroughly stoned.

Some months earlier, when talking to my friend Christine, I'd mentioned the choir and our fun warm-ups.

'Will you run a singing workshop at Uluru?' she asked me. 'I'm taking a group there in November'.

Christine suggested I do warm-up exercises with the group members, and teach them a song that would be performed, recorded and put on YouTube at the end of the five-day cultural and educational program. I felt a bit fearful at the prospect, but my gut feeling was to say yes. So I accepted. I considered a number of songs and nothing seemed suitable. So I wrote some words myself, and asked Graeme to set them to music. I had just enough money in the bank to pay for my fare and accommodation. The NSW Trustee & Guardian agreed to paying for Graeme to attend, as money he'd inherited from his father had gone into his account with them. So we decided to do the trip and the workshop together.

JUST AN ORDINARY PERSON

I remember being full of anxiety about my sessions with the group. But they were lovely people, and we enjoyed all the activities together—dot painting, drawing mandalas, visiting Kata Tjuta (previously known as the Olgas) as well as Uluru (Ayers Rock). We'd expected to have the famous 'Sounds of Silence' evening meal under the stars, but within minutes of our arrival at the beautifully set up venue—as we were offered canapés and chilled sparkling wine—the heavens opened! Absolutely drenched, we had to return to our coach and be driven back to our accommodation. My white shoes were saturated with red mud.

The performance of the song wasn't good enough to be shared on the internet, but it rounded off an enjoyable and educational visit to Australia's centre.

***

Richard remarried before I left Barraba. In fact, he and his wife visited me there and all four of us drove together to Armidale to sing in that year's choral festival. Richard had previously sung in a few of them. He had a fine tenor voice. (He'd got his scholarship to university because of his singing voice.) But Richard had developed diabetes and had serious problems with his feet. He ended up in Barraba hospital after that trip to Armidale.

At the end of 2012, he was diagnosed with a kidney problem and, a few weeks after that, was admitted to hospital for surgery to clear a blocked kidney duct. He died, quite unexpectedly, within hours of the operation. We'd been in regular contact through emails and phone calls, and Richard had his iPad in the hospital with him. Just before surgery he had sent me an email in which he recommended tapping therapy, saying it had been helpful to him. He hadn't been aware of the fact that I'd attended online 'Tapping Summits' for some years and was most familiar with the technique. He died on 12 February 2013, exactly one month after the birth of Simon's second son.

* * *

That year I was in charge of a community garden in Umina, where half a dozen of us had been growing our herbs and veggies. The many trees, the local wildlife and the lack of fences between properties in Pearl Beach made it impossible to do at home. I was also visiting my grandsons once a week. I'd previously travelled down twice a week to look after Simon's firstborn for the second year of his life, his mother having returned to work. Now, I wanted to keep in touch, so I spent each Wednesday with him. I would take him to his local library's singing and craft session before picnicking and playing in a beautifully designed nearby park.

As mentioned earlier, my seventy-ninth birthday was a turning point. I'd taken on so much that I was anxious about meeting my commitments—pleasurable as they were. I felt so strongly the need to step back from it all that in May 2014, I gave notice that I would be giving up all my voluntary commitments at the end of the year.

Soon afterwards, a friend who'd suffered a severe stroke phoned and asked me if I could help her for an hour or two, a couple of days a week. She'd just come out of hospital and needed someone to take her blood pressure each morning and evening, and drive her to medical appointments. She had a professional carer for the other five days. I was very happy to be paid to help on Tuesdays and Thursdays; and I did enjoy my six months with her. But, as time passed, our duties and times changed greatly. We still recorded the blood pressure and drove to medical appointments, of which there were many—optometrist, neurologist, chiropodist, general practitioner. But my friend revelled in having her two carers at her beck and call. We never knew what we would be asked to do, where we would be going, or for how long she would require our services, as she worked through a kind of bucket list. Some days, I arrived at 7 am and didn't leave until 5:30.

I not only dealt with the 850 unopened emails and numerous Facebook messages I initially found on her iPad, but I cleaned countless copper saucepans and their lids at her request—or should I say 'command'. I don't think anyone ever said no to this lady. She was charm and grace personified, and we were only too happy to assist her.

One job I wasn't asked to do a second time, though, was letter writing. My first 'Thank You' card to a nurse at the hospital was met with,

'Dee, can't you write more slowly and make it look better? We were taught copperplate when I was at school'.

BESIDE THE SEASIDE, BESIDE THE SEA

I was glad I failed this task, as the other carer ended up writing dozens of letters to her many, many friends and family members—in a perfect copperplate hand.

There was one day that I'll never forget. The previous night, a Sunday, I'd travelled by car, two trains and a water-taxi to a wonderful performance of the opera *Aida* on Sydney Harbour. With no commitments the next day, I wasn't too disappointed when I missed the train from Central by two minutes and had to wait another fifty-eight minutes on the cold and windy platform before arriving home at 1:30 am. But the next morning was not the late and leisurely start I'd expected. At ten to seven I was summoned. I was woken with news that the other carer was sick and I was to be there at seven. So, bed unmade and shower-less, I hurriedly dressed and drove around. I said nothing about my late night, but this was the day that my friend wanted lots of jobs done.

After making the queen-sized bed, washing up, brushing crumbs off the beautiful aqua carpet, hanging out the washing and sweeping the possum poo off the large back deck, there was an enormous round window to be cleaned. To reach the top of it, I had to stand on a heavy wooden stool. The cloths I was given were shiny and unsuitable and, as I worked, the window looked dirtier than when I'd started. I sneaked a bit of paper towelling from the kitchen and redid the inside. I then carried the awkward and heavy stool outside and along the narrow space between the house and the fence to clean the outside of the window. Oh, dear! It seemed the inside was still smeary. I went in and out, in and out, carrying that heavy stool each time—and still it didn't look good. Talk about frustration! In the end, I said I'd done the best I could, and put away the cleaner, the cloths and the stool.

I'd noticed that a mop I'd brought along some weeks earlier was sitting in a bucket of water in the garage. This was one of those modern mop and bucket items where you rinse, then spin-dry the mop head by pushing its handle up and down vigorously. I'd bought it for myself, but hadn't ever used it and, on discovering that her garage roof let in the rain, I'd offered it to my friend. Today, I suggested that it not be left in the water. Her response was to drive the car out of the garage so I could mop the entire lino floor. After reading the instructions, and some trial and error, I painstakingly mopped it all twice—once with detergent in the water, then again with clean water. Some marks didn't budge, and when I mentioned this, I was informed that when her husband was alive, he kept it absolutely spotless—and the next moment she appeared with a piece of steel wool and a bottle of Ajax for me to use on the stubborn stains. On hands and knees I did what I could, then mopped the whole area again.

I actually managed to get out of the next job I was asked to do. My friend was a lover of prawns, oysters and other seafood, and her just-emptied rubbish bin absolutely stank! My stomach turns now just thinking about it. She asked me to clean it out! I suggested the gardener/handyman do it when he came that afternoon; I knew he usually cleaned the bins. And so, after I'd swept all the brick paving between the garage and the road, my services were no longer required. I took myself home, had something to eat, did my own daily jobs, then returned for the evening duties. I went to bed early that night, as the next day I was due to be on duty again at 7 am.

* * *

As my community work lessened and my income increased, I was going to ballet, operas and theatre again—the choir had given me a generous gift-voucher for the Opera House. I also did more reading, and came across Marie Kondo's wonderful book on tidying up. I spent many months going through every one of my possessions, tidying, sorting, cleaning and clearing, rolling my clothes, and colour-coordinating everything in my wardrobe. I began the New Year 2015 full of expectations. I'd decided to learn circular breathing so I could play the Jew's harp expertly. I would get my book of verses published. I had so many plans.

But in early January I did a three-day online retreat! Over a period of a week, I sat at my computer in my free time and joined a small group of men and women on retreat at the Findhorn Foundation in Scotland. This special event had taken place over three days in December, and I'd paid to participate through online video recordings of all the sessions. Initially, I was not at all impressed. The leader, Jeff Foster, had prepared nothing, and said very little, very slowly. If I hadn't paid so much I would not have kept watching it. But thankfully, I continued, and I ended up with a completely new understanding of what it means to be living in the 'present moment'.

I was already aware of the benefits of meditation, of mindfulness, of being in the present. In fact my favourite sayings included

JUST AN ORDINARY PERSON

The greatest way to freedom is to feel your feelings and *The present is the best gift of all*. (I actually wrote them on bookmarks when I was learning calligraphy while living in Katoomba.) But by the end of my online retreat, I no longer needed the 108 list, and I no longer had agendas in regard to other people, whether family or politicians or those we hear about in the news. I'd decided to put into practice what I had learned—to stop anticipating what I might say or do in coming situations, stop wishing, stop judging, stop planning, stop trying to change things. To notice but not give attention to my mind as it tried to find solutions to everything; to gently bring my attention back to my breathing and to what I was experiencing with my senses—even if it wasn't what I wanted. And it gave me a whole new outlook on how best to help Graeme, and a better understanding of my estranged relationship with Wendy—she still lived in London and had sent a card when I moved to Pearl Beach. In it, she wished me well, but said she was not comfortable communicating with me.

After that 'retreat' it was so strange at first. I was used to planning and making to-do lists. Now I was learning to be completely spontaneous. But I did enjoy starting most days with no idea of what, if anything, I would do. And there was the added bonus of no more procrastination and the uncomfortable guilt that comes with it. You can't put off what you haven't planned to do! It was a totally new experience for me to do whatever I felt like doing, with no limits and no judgement.

The most surprising thing was that I found myself doing so much. With the pressure off, my automatic pilot had me cleaning, clearing, sorting and socialising as I'd never done before. Ideas just came to me. It was as if I were a radio, now tuned to a different station or frequency. The almost constant chatter, judgements, regrets and anxieties had been replaced by beauty, love and contentment. I had the best year.

Then, completely out of the blue, in January 2016, came the news that the little cabin I'd expected to be in for life was being sold. I had to move. I had no savings left, only a pension income, and I'd been paying the tiniest rent. I was in a state of shock but had a sense that this was a gift to me, and an opportunity to test my new values and beliefs.

And the next two-and-a-half months were extraordinary. I had the intention and expectation of finding the perfect place—something affordable, attractive, close to public transport and, most importantly, a place where I could grow my own veggies and herbs. And that is what I got. Not planning or worrying actually allowed the most incredible things to happen.

First of all my Canberra friend, Barbara, invited me to look at some inexpensive and most suitable accommodation she knew about, so I immediately went down to Canberra and spent some productive days with her, putting in an application for their waiting list. I didn't really want to be that far from my family, but it was comforting to have a backup plan. Barbara also helped me look up rental properties online and printed out application forms for me.

My friend Judy had already left Pearl Beach and was living in the Blue Mountains close to her daughter and grandchild. She had a sense that I might be moving to the mountains again. So I added that area to my real estate app, and looked at possible places there. I found a lovely brick granny flat, where the landlords lived in the attached house. It was close to public transport, which was a big plus as I needed to sell my car to make ends meet. The interior was in excellent condition, and through every window there were views of native trees and shrubs. Most importantly, the enclosed backyard had plenty of room for veggie growing.

A neighbour in Pearl Beach offered me an unlimited supply of packing cases and white butcher paper for packing. I sold, through Gumtree, some items of furniture that wouldn't fit in the new place. In every case, the first person to phone came and paid in cash the full amount I'd asked for, and took the item away on the spot. When I had a garage sale, my next-door neighbour just happened to have six beautifully written signs directing people from the main road—he'd kept them and their attachments after his garage sale months earlier. The man opposite me bought my car—I merely parked it on the other side of the road the day before my move, signed some forms and handed him the key. The other 'carer' helped me pack, and cleaned the house thoroughly after my departure. And the sun shone on moving day despite the forecast of rain!

It had been a busy time, of course, as I sorted and packed and made all the necessary arrangements for the move, but the whole experience was an enjoyable one. There were no difficulties at all, and those months were absolute proof to me of the value of living in the present and expecting the best.

CHAPTER 16

BACK IN THE BEAUTIFUL BLUE MOUNTAINS

My move from Pearl Beach to Woodford in the Blue Mountains was a DIY one. To keep costs down, Simon hired a small truck, and he and Martin did the loading and unloading. Graeme was to have helped that day but was a 'no show'.

At my new home I quickly unpacked my many boxes. My landlord Bernie, a lovely Cornish man a bit older than me, was skilled in many trades. When I asked permission to hang my pictures, he provided the fittings and did the job for me. He also provided many of the materials I needed for my veggie gardens—bricks, netting and stakes. He and his wife were happy for me to make garden beds anywhere except in the middle of the lawn, and it wasn't long before I had no-dig beds along all three boundary fences and on two sides of the garden shed, with additional pots of herbs on the patio beside my outdoor table and chairs and large hammock. There were possums in his roof, so my beds needed covering at night.

The morning after my arrival, as I relaxed in the sun between unpacking jobs, Bernie handed me the local paper and I read about a free class for people interested in writing about their life. Friends had often said to me, 'You should write a book' after hearing some of my stories, so now seemed a good opportunity. I immediately phoned and booked a place. There was also to be a course on 'growing your own garlic', so I booked for that one, too. The writing group actually met every month, and it provided an opportunity for us to write on a set subject, then read our story aloud; there were no comments on what was written, but the topics were most interesting. We began by drawing the area in which we grew up, and writing about each room in our house. We were led by English-born John Hockney, youngest brother of painter David Hockney. His warmth and support and acceptance made it a comfortable and happy group.

At the time of my move, I'd missed buying my usual TV guide, so I bought a Monday Sydney Morning Herald newspaper knowing it included the week's TV programs. I never buy newspapers, but I looked through this one and, lo and behold, on page three I saw a large colour photograph of a former Pearl Beach friend. She was now living fifteen minutes away from me, and the article was about her involvement with a local Timebanking system.

BACK IN THE BEAUTIFUL BLUE MOUNTAINS

I'd learned that the Blue Mountains LETS no longer existed. Timebanking was another way that people were sharing their skills and time with one another. So I went online and joined the local group, offering piano lessons. I noticed that some months previously, a recently retired woman had listed a request for lessons. I contacted her to ask if she was still looking for a teacher. She was, and we made arrangements to meet at a local cafe to discuss it. But the following day, I was phoned by the Timebanking organiser and asked if SBS TV could film me pretending to give her a piano lesson! They were doing a segment on Timebanking for 'The Feed'. It was scary, but I said yes. A time was arranged, I prepared some material for the 'lesson' and I baked a cake to offer everyone when it was over.

My new pupil and I met for the first time with a camera following our every move. Such a strange experience, but it created a bond, and we continued with the lessons and became good friends.

My friend Judy had visited me a couple of days after my arrival in Woodford with goodies from her garden. She'd then driven me to the food co-op in Katoomba and shown me the community gardens and the charity shop before taking me to lunch, then the supermarket, and driving me home. Her friendship and generosity were wonderful as I settled into an area far away from most of my friends and family.

I was still travelling each week to spend time with my young grandsons, now two hours away by public transport. I was giving formal piano lessons to the oldest one. Through Timebanking I had four other pupils visiting me at home.

In a new area, with no car, and my income just covering rent and food, I felt my 'wings had been clipped'. But I was more comfortable and content than I'd ever been. I loved gardening and being able to walk out my back door to tend or harvest my veggies.

Before the move I'd looked online for information on local choirs. There were many of them, but rehearsals were usually at night. With no nighttime buses and an hourly train service, the idea of evening rehearsals on cold winter nights kept me from joining. I continued to attend the Armidale annual choral weekend, and also went to a couple of one-off singing events—one where we prepared and performed Handel's 'Messiah'.

When I read that the wonderful music educator Richard Gill was to form and conduct a Flash Mob Choir at Sydney's City Recital Hall, I wanted to be part of it. But the first one was scheduled for 8 am. (The times were chosen so that Sydney workers could attend before or after work, or in their lunch breaks.) So, well before 6 o'clock that morning I was sitting on the seat at Woodford station awaiting the city train. A couple came and sat beside me. He was heading for work, but I overheard her saying that she was going to the Flash Mob Choir. I introduced myself and we travelled together and chatted. She invited me to join the choir that she sang in, and offered to take me there and back each week. It was wonderful. My new friend made photocopies of the music for me to look at in advance and, for the first time in nearly seventy years, I was again singing in an all-female choir. Our brilliant conductor arranged a variety of music for four-part women's voices. I was introduced to a whole new repertoire of music.

* * *

When Graeme first appeared in Woodford I decided that he was not to stay overnight unless invited. I was just three minutes from a railway station, and he was within walking distance at the other end. I always found the smell of his smoke-drenched and unwashed clothes offensive, and his usual behaviour was to arrive very late at night, extremely hungry, out of food (and out of money, of course) and with a backpack full of very dirty clothes. I sometimes felt I was 'being used'. I'd always thought it was best not to allow people to 'eat their cake and have it, too'. In Barraba there'd been band members who always fed Graeme when he'd gambled all his money, and I'd disapproved, believing it was not helpful in the long run.

But I also believed in the Golden Rule of treating others as you'd like to be treated—the Christian idea of seeing the Christ in everyone. I remember an occasion when I was staying in Findhorn back in the mid-1980s. Having recently become a Christian, I was definitely into treating everyone as I would treat Jesus. Two visiting VIP 'speakers', both ministers of religion, needed a lift from one venue to another a few miles away. I'd offered to drive them there. It was pouring with rain and, as we travelled, we passed a tramp-like man and his dog clearly wanting a lift. I immediately stopped and invited them into the car, much to the quiet amazement of my passengers.

At Woodford I chose to respond to Graeme as I would to a truly welcome visitor. But I must admit I would 'freeze' inside when the outside sensor light came on while I was relaxing late at night, watching an absorbing TV program, and I felt so relieved if it was just a neighbour's cat. If it was Graeme, I'd switch off the TV, give him a hug and prepare a meal while he got out of the clothes he'd been wearing for days and nights (Graeme slept in his clothes at home). He'd shower, wash his hair and put on the clean clothes I always kept at my place, before sitting down to eat. I'd put all his dirty clothes in the washing machine, and make up the sofa bed. After ravenously eating, he'd go outside for a couple of cigarettes before going to bed. I'd clean up in the kitchen, hang the wet clothes on racks, then go to bed myself. At that time I usually listened to music on the radio in bed, especially if I woke during the night. And I liked to turn the radio on first thing in the morning. But even if the volume was low, Graeme would call from the other room as the slightest sound of music disturbed him. He would sleep the whole of the next day and night, when possible. If I had a piano pupil coming, we'd move his bedding to the large hammock outside so I could get the room back to normal. He'd then go for a walk before my pupil arrived, and come back once they'd left.

Graeme never bought or used drugs at any time when he was with me. There were occasions when he stayed for some days, and we had lovely bush walks together, played piano, he sang, and we played Scrabble as we ate our meals together. These were the times when we'd take the train to Penrith, have his hair cut and buy clothing from Lowes. I would get approval from the Trustee & Guardian, send them the receipts and be reimbursed from Graeme's money. Whenever there was a Monday public holiday, his pension for the whole week was paid to him on the Thursday night. That meant he would then be without food and money for a whole week, and he would have had a larger than usual amount of marijuana and 'ice'. I was never surprised when he appeared late Thursday night before a long weekend.

For some years, Graeme had been in need of dental work. He had such a fear of dentists that he just didn't turn up for appointments and he'd been banned from using the free pensioner dental services. By 2017, he'd lost so many teeth that arrangements were made for me to go with him to a private dentist very close to where Graeme lived. He would come up and stay with me the night before his appointment and we'd travel back there by train together. He needed to have most of his teeth out, and plates fitted. But it wasn't long before our system broke down. Graeme failed to come to my place. If I did manage to go down and get him to the dentist's, treatment often wasn't possible due to the drugs he'd taken. Evidently anaesthetics for extractions have no effect on someone who has recently had marijuana. The dentist would send him home and we'd make another appointment. Plates were made, but Graeme found them uncomfortable and didn't wear them. The dental work came to a halt, though the dentist and I were still communicating and endeavouring to get Graeme to continue with his treatment.

JUST AN ORDINARY PERSON

Then in late October 2017, Graeme had an accident. The police thought it was a suicide attempt when they phoned me at 3:30 that morning. Graeme had broken both ankles when he fell or jumped from his second-floor balcony. He was in hospital and would need surgery. By 6:30 am I was there with him as X-rays were being taken. Graeme was in good spirits. He was so accepting of what I would regard as difficulties. He told me he hadn't tried to kill himself. He'd been high on drugs and, feeling invincible, jumped off the balcony. He borrowed my iPhone to make some calls, and asked me to buy him a mobile phone as an early birthday/Christmas present. So I went off as soon as the shops were open and got one for him.

I visited him several times during the next few days, as did his brother Martin. Martin surprised us all by travelling by public transport after work each night, bringing magazines, chocolates and fruit. He lived and worked well north of Sydney, and the hospital was south of the city.

I had many conversations with Graeme's mental health case worker, the social worker at the hospital, the doctor in charge, the physiotherapist and others. We all agreed Graeme should remain in hospital for six weeks after the surgery, as he would be confined to a bed or wheelchair for that period of time. My granny flat wasn't wheelchair-friendly; it wouldn't have been possible for him to get to the bathroom at my place.

While I was now accepting of Graeme's problems, I still had the expectation that he would overcome them and be able to live the kind of life he often talked of—marrying, having children, having a successful job, being part of our family again. So, I was thinking this enforced time away from drugs and gambling might be the rehab that he needed.

But it wasn't to be. After his surgery, Graeme insisted on leaving the hospital and returning to his flat. He'd persuaded them that he could manage by himself in a wheelchair. I could hardly believe it when I arrived to visit three days after his operations and was told he'd been discharged.

I visited Graeme at his flat. He couldn't even get his wheelchair in or out of his front door without help. He'd done deals with a neighbour who would visit him at 6 o'clock each morning and make him coffee, and with a former neighbour, R—an often violent man whose mother and sister both had AVOs against him, and who'd previously assaulted Graeme a number of times. R would push the wheelchair up the hill so Graeme could get to the shops.

Graeme had been given injections to use daily to prevent clotting, which could easily result from inactivity. He was continuing to use 'ice' and marijuana, the dealers now coming to him. He told me the true story of his accident—after a late-night session of drug-taking with a number of his friends and their dealer, the dealer had fallen asleep. Graeme, on a high and feeling he could take on the world, took $1,000 worth of ice from the dealer's pocket, then jumped off his second-floor balcony and attempted to run off with it.

JUST AN ORDINARY PERSON

I'd been to Graeme's place many times through the years. I actually disliked being there. A few times I'd done a 'spring clean', one of them with help from Martin. The large windows, the bathroom, the fridge and the carpets were only cleaned when we did them, and I'd decided not to do it again. When Graeme was in the hospital I'd offered to make arrangements for an 'end of lease' complete clean, so he could return to a more comfortable and attractive place. I'd even talked of his moving to new premises. He had not been interested in any of that, and was now endeavouring to care for himself in filthy, cockroach-infested rooms. The bedroom window had been smashed and not repaired. There were still pieces of broken glass along one side of his bed. But it was his choice. His need to smoke, gamble and use the drugs that made him feel so good, overrode any good judgement.

After returning home from the hospital, Graeme kept hocking his latest phone. But I managed to speak to him a few times, and continued visiting.

* * *

Back when he'd first inherited money from his father, Graeme had planned to take me on a cruise to New Zealand. We'd gone together to a travel agent when I lived in Pearl Beach and had made plans, but not a commitment. When the money came through, instead of it going directly to Graeme's account with the Trustee & Guardian, it remained in our joint account over the weekend. During that time, even though the bank had agreed to cancel his card, Graeme succeeded in withdrawing over $4,000. He'd bought a cup of coffee and had gone by taxi to the casino in Sydney, where every cent of it was lost. So, it didn't seem a good time to apply for $6,000 to be made available for him to go with me on a cruise.

But when Martin phoned me prior to Graeme's accident and invited me to go on a cruise holiday with him, I thought of the New Zealand one. Martin had saved money while living with his step-grandmother, and wanted company for an overseas holiday. I'd thought my days of going on holidays were long past. I happily accepted Martin's offer and made a booking for a New Zealand cruise for the following January. We finalised arrangements at my place on 6 December, when Martin visited me to celebrate his fifty-seventh birthday with a high tea at the famous Medlow Bath Hydro Majestic Hotel.

I'd spoken to Graeme by phone the night before, the Tuesday. He'd borrowed a phone to call me. Having missed his follow-up appointment at the hospital, he was now to go there on Friday—his forty-third birthday. We had planned to celebrate that day with a special picnic meal at a nearby park, so I now suggested that I meet him at the hospital and then after his appointment we'd have a special meal together. Graeme had known about the cruise and wanted to come with us. He was sure he'd be recovered by then. But he was having great difficulty managing, and told me of painfully dragging himself up a flight of stairs in order to get to the poker machines. He also said that R was no longer willing to push him up the hill to the shops. And there were cockroaches inside the plaster on both legs.

JUST AN ORDINARY PERSON

'I must have had rocks in my head, when I said I could manage here by myself', he said.

I was glad we were soon to talk to the hospital staff, and I looked forward to seeing Graeme on the Friday morning.

On Thursday afternoon I was at home, chatting to my friend Judy. I'd asked her to call in for her birthday present. My phone rang, and I answered it straight away as I could see it was from Graeme's friend R.

'Graeme's dead!' he said. 'Graeme's dead!' He was most upset and hard to understand. But I got the message. A group of them had been together at Graeme's place and had had lots of drugs. At one point Graeme said he felt unwell, and took himself, in his wheelchair, to the bathroom. Hours later, someone came to the door asking for Graeme. The others realised he'd not come out of the bathroom, and went in there to find him on the floor, unconscious. R tried resuscitation to no avail. Someone called the police. Most of them disappeared. R had stayed until the police arrived.

I got more information and a rather different version from the policeman in charge when he rang me soon afterwards. I never got to meet this wonderful man personally, but he stayed in touch with me until after the coroner's report came through eleven months later. He'd given me his mobile phone number, and from the beginning he could not have been more helpful or more considerate.

BACK IN THE BEAUTIFUL BLUE MOUNTAINS

And I'm so thankful that Judy was with me when I got the news. She knew Graeme well, knew of our relationship, and was the perfect person to be there for me at the time.

Along with my shock and surprise that Graeme was dead, I felt immediate relief that his difficulties had come to an end. And I was aware that I would be inheriting the sizeable sum of money he had with the Trustee & Guardian. I'd known that in NSW if someone dies without making a will, and without a spouse or children, that their estate then goes to their parents. I would be sole beneficiary.

A shock and the accompanying adrenaline rush has always brought out the best in me. In this instance, there was much to be done and I was only too ready to take it on. The days that followed were extraordinary, but I cruised along comfortably as seemingly unbelievable things occurred.

I notified all the people who needed to be notified—family here and in England, Graeme's case worker, the hospital, the Department of Housing, the Trustee & Guardian, CentreLink, etc. I looked up on my phone what steps needed to be taken after a death, and I went through them all systematically. My email to Wendy bounced back as there was an error in the address I had. Sadly, neither she nor her now twenty-three-year-old daughter have been in contact with any of us for some years now—though I'm still in touch with my former son-in-law, Paul. I asked one of her daughter's Facebook friends to pass on the news.

JUST AN ORDINARY PERSON

Graeme died Thursday afternoon, 7 December 2017. On Friday I travelled to Simon's place and discussed things with him and Martin, who took the day off work. We decided on a small Sydney funeral and a private cremation, the dates to be decided once the body was released. On Saturday we all met up again at Graeme's flat. Fortunately I'd kept a spare key the last time his locks were changed. We spent the day going through every item in the apartment. Simon concentrated on the 'papers' and found unpaid bills and letters from debt collectors. It appeared Graeme had 'bought' then sold, unused, at least one iPhone. He owed thousands of dollars to each of the three main telcos. With the Trustee & Guardian managing Graeme's finances we'd not expected unpaid bills. But here were also notices of unpaid fines from court hearings for drug possession, for travelling by rail without a ticket, and for petty theft.

We sorted through everything—emptied every kitchen cupboard, the fridge, the bathroom cabinet. The broken wheelchair belonged to the hospital, so I phoned and made arrangements for its return. We filled many large rubbish bags. Nothing was worth keeping apart from the bills, some music manuscripts and notebooks.

There was no way we could possibly clean the flat ourselves. I decided to arrange for an 'end of lease' company to remove the old bed, lounge and other furniture and do a thorough clean. How appreciative I was when I rang the Department of Housing first thing on the Monday morning and was told that all I needed to do now was meet them at Graeme's flat and give them the key. They would deal with the clearing, the cleaning and any necessary repairs.

BACK IN THE BEAUTIFUL BLUE MOUNTAINS

That week I made five trips to Sydney, travel taking at least two hours each way. But I didn't feel tired at all. At home I listened to some beautiful and moving music on CDs—my favourite being a selection of cello and orchestral arrangements that included 'Time to Say Goodbye' and 'Dido's Lament'. I had no desire to turn on the TV or radio until several days after the funeral. I was eating well and going to bed early. I often woke at about 2 am, but I'd then use my phone to research funeral directors, services, and administration of estates, before going to sleep again. I slept well.

Friends seemed to phone or text me at the perfect time. I'd posted a notice of Graeme's death on my Facebook page, and found the response from my friends was enormously helpful. I could feel their love supporting me. I had so many friends in Pearl Beach that I considered the possibility of holding a get-together there in the new year to celebrate Graeme's life.

Watering the garden and tending it, and harvesting and preparing my meals was 'nurturing'. I reread a book I'd had for years on grief counselling and I gave myself permission to feel whatever emotions arose, be comfortable with whatever thoughts came into my head, and do whatever I needed to do as I moved through this unexpected and major experience of loss.

On the Sunday, I sorted through all the boxes of family photos and chose ones of Graeme to use in a slideshow. On the Monday, Simon went with me to the funeral home I'd selected. It was quite surreal choosing the coffin, the decorations and flowers, refreshments and brochure for the simple ceremony we'd chosen.

JUST AN ORDINARY PERSON

But now I want to tell you about some of the 'weird' or extraordinary things that happened in the days after Graeme's death. I began listing them all on a large red envelope I had in my desk. But they happened all the time, and there was no way I could keep recording them all.

Graeme was always interested in what he called 'the afterlife'. He and I both seemed to be able to communicate with what we would call 'spirit guides' and with people who had passed on. Richard, too, had that ability. So did my mother's father.

Ever since I contacted an inner voice at a Findhorn workshop in 1987, I've 'tuned in' most mornings and asked for guidance 'from the highest'. Wherever it's coming from, it's been extremely helpful. On the Sunday after Graeme's death, I woke very early and got up to find that the large vase of flowers on top of the piano was now lying on its side—the flowers on the floor, and water over the piano keys and on the floor. They were flowers from my garden that I'd picked the morning after Graeme's death. I'd placed a studio photograph of him next to the vase. It had been there, untouched, for two days. I cleaned it all up and did a thorough clean of the piano, then went back to bed and back to sleep. When I next woke, I picked up my journal and tuned in as usual to my 'guides'. Instead of the expected *'Greetings, Diane,'* this is what I received:

Graeme here, Mum!

It's so beautiful here!

BACK IN THE BEAUTIFUL BLUE MOUNTAINS

Yes, Dad's with me and we're having a few laughs—same sense of humour—he really laughs at my jokes.

I'm thanking God that I'm free. Thank you and Simon and Martin for everything you did for me—for your love—and for yesterday's work. Not a nice job to have to do.

Of course I'm sorry for what I put you all through. But it had to be. There's no two ways about it.

Do you want to know about the flowers? I did that (as you immediately thought). Keep the piano keys clean, Mum. And play more often. And maybe today get out the photos of me and take them to Simon's. He can do the 'copying' of them to digital.

I do love you, Mum. As much as Dad does. We both adore you, but had to give you a hard time—sometimes. It was at your request, you could say.

Don't worry about my musical compositions, but you could have fun trying to play them.

Please tell all your friends that I've connected with you. A lot of them don't understand the afterlife—I didn't.

Everyone is here— Willy Wally, Grandma .... yes, JL, granny, Tina and Cliff and Dad you know about. But many more who love me and are rejoicing in my new life.

I'm free, Mum! You used to tell me about this life being about learning about freedom, money and my physical body. Well, you and the clairvoyant were right. But we didn't understand that the way I learned the value of them was by not having them. I didn't suffer the way you thought I did. I did what I had to do.

So, Mum, never ever try to get someone to change—or even offer to help them change. It can make it harder for them to 'play their role,' as you would put it.

Haha! I'm the wise one now.

But as you know, Mum, I've always loved your healings, which you gave me whenever I asked.

Do more healing work, but with no agenda at all. You've no idea how powerful that kind of healing is, and how helpful to someone who is in pain of any sort.

Mum, have no regrets—about anything.

Tell Marty he was wonderful after my accident. We clashed a lot, I know, but I really loved both my brothers, as well as Giles and Clare, and all the family in England.

I am feeling their love.

Go ahead with the Pearl Beach plans—it can be called a Memorial, because it will be about memories. Thank you for involving me in your productions. It was so helpful for me to spend time with the choir and all the others in Pearl Beach and Barraba. And I truly was proud of everything you did with the youth clubs and shows and everything like that. You were not only the Queen of Upwords!

BACK IN THE BEAUTIFUL BLUE MOUNTAINS

Mum, you've got a while to go yet, and there's a lot you can still do to help other people and to help yourself.

Enjoy spending my money! You'll make much better use of it than I did.

Sorry about the debts—but there'll be plenty left over for you to enjoy.

I'll be with you and Marty on the ship to New Zealand. Haha! It was all my idea!

Offer spiritual healing on the new LETS-type group you've joined. You wouldn't have known about it, except through what I did.

R, P, even W and G were all good souls (like me) playing their roles.

So no judgement at all, Mum, on anyone, anytime.

Everyone is doing what they have to do—whether they like it or not.

Maybe I should write a book!

I could dictate it to you!

Sorry I didn't complete the accompaniments/music for your verses, and the Uluru song is not really completed.

JUST AN ORDINARY PERSON

But to quote you, 'You'll know what you have to do, when you have to do it!'

OVER AND OUT FOR NOW,

Gra

I continued to feel Graeme's presence—and still do, much of the time—but in the days after that 'communication' it appeared to me that he was having fun exploring 'new powers'. Many were to do with my phone. There was the call from Simon with no sound and no vibration. My phone calendar said it was 11 December when it was the 12th. The phone would always seize up or freeze when it was time for me to stop a conversation. On one occasion I looked at my phone and it said 'You're recording a message'. An email I'd read was then shown as unread.

Other strange events included all the boxes in the shed falling down, the kitchen clock being thirty-five minutes slow, a nail file falling off a ledge, and my bag falling over in the train and again on the seat on the platform. And, on that first Monday, I had the most unusual train trip to Sydney. My train arrived twenty minutes late, then stopped at every station, not just the scheduled ones. At Strathfield, where I was to change from platform three to platform six, the noticeboard showed that my train would now depart from platform three. So back I went, and waited, and waited. The platform sign was going berserk. Eventually there was an announcement that the train expected on platform three would now depart from platform six. So off we all went again down the ramp and elevator. The train unexpectedly terminated at Rhodes, two stops before the one I needed. Eventually another train arrived, and I reached my destination ninety minutes later than expected.

A very helpful 'message' from Graeme came the following week. I'd originally told R that he'd be welcome to attend Graeme's funeral. I hadn't known at the time that he was the person who had threatened Simon and his family years back. No way did Simon want that man at the service. I told R that we'd decided on a family-only funeral service. He had been sending me text messages ever since Graeme's death. They'd begun with him mentioning his love for Graeme, his 'brother'. He told me he had been Graeme's carer and had paid his debts and was owed money. I responded with gratitude but didn't offer to reimburse him, as I was in debt myself. He then outright asked me for half of Graeme's estate. I ignored that text and he became most abusive, eventually sending a very nasty message saying he'd take me to court if I didn't give him half the inheritance.

I was unsettled, and not sure how to respond. I decided to put it out of my mind for the time being, and went into the garden and began watering the plants. At one stage I directed a thought to Graeme. 'What should I say to R?'

I was surprised to receive a very clear answer.

'Tell R that Graeme has a message for him. The message is 'R, stop bothering my Mum!'

JUST AN ORDINARY PERSON

So I went inside and I sent a text to R. I said that since Graeme's death he had communicated with me, and 'today he gave me a message for you'. I added the message, and pressed send. I never heard from R again

Graeme's funeral was attended by Simon, his wife and two young sons, Martin, my sister's two oldest sons, and some friends of Simon's from university days who'd known Graeme well when he lived with Simon. It was a DIY service. Simon welcomed everyone, I gave the eulogy, a recording of Debussy's 'Clair De Lune' was played, there was a poem I'd chosen, and the slideshow. And I read the 'Letter from Graeme'. A moving version of 'Time To Say Goodbye' was played as we left the chapel and gathered together for conversation and refreshments. Tea, coffee and biscuits had been set up, but it was an extremely hot day and iced water was what we all chose.

After leaving the building, the family had an enjoyable meal together at a nearby restaurant. It had been many years since I'd seen my nephews and the wife and children of the younger one. I'd attempted to get us all together for my eightieth birthday, but without success. My sister's oldest son lived in Queensland. Before Graeme's death, he had planned to be in Sydney the weekend before Christmas, and we'd all arranged to meet up for a picnic and swim on the Saturday. It was fortuitous that the coroner released Graeme's body in time for us to have the funeral instead of the picnic that day, and that my two nephews could be there.

BACK IN THE BEAUTIFUL BLUE MOUNTAINS

But it was a strange day for me. I was aware that usually the mother of a deceased person would be picked up at home and driven to the funeral. I travelled alone by train and bus to Central Station, as trackwork was being carried out that weekend. Then I took another bus to the funeral director's. I was early, but Martin soon arrived, and we sat on a seat in the morning sun until it was time to go into the building. Afterwards, I'd arranged to stay the night at Simon's place. I went back there with him in his car, but felt fine about continuing home. So Simon walked me to the bus stop and I caught a bus to Parramatta, a railway bus to Penrith, then the train. All had gone smoothly and comfortably.

***

I organised the memorial service for Graeme in the appropriately named Memorial Hall at Pearl Beach for mid-January. A close friend of mine offered to set up the hall. Friends who had a catering business prepared a delicious afternoon tea, and another good friend handled the sound and the slideshow. This time, as well as the eulogy, I gave a twenty-minute commentary as the slides of Graeme were shown. And this time, I was driven to and from the venue. My piano pupil and friend Barbara had generously offered to drive me all the way from the Blue Mountains to Pearl Beach, but Judy wanted to attend, so it was she who picked me up and took me there.

Simon, his wife and children, and Martin all came. There were about eighty people there to celebrate Graeme's life. It was the most lovely experience for me to be back in that hall where I'd had so many happy times, and to meet again with dear friends, some of whom had been very fond of Graeme. It was nearly two years since I'd left, and I was glad to have the opportunity of moving around and talking to everyone, before and after the 'formalities'.

The following week, Martin and I set off on our New Zealand cruise. We felt Graeme was with us and sharing our enjoyment. (Strangely, the first person to sit beside me at the dinner table was a singer and trombone player called Graeme.) Our ship had left Sydney one day late, due to extremely rough seas on its previous trip. But for our entire trip the water was calm, the sky was clear and at every port we had unusually good weather.

After our return, Simon and Martin came up to my place with Graeme's ashes. We did the three-kilometre bush walk to a hidden waterfall in the National Park at Woodford. It was a favourite place of Graeme's. He used to go there with school friends when living in Katoomba, and he'd taken me there when I moved to Woodford. We had a picnic lunch and scattered Graeme's ashes. On the way home we stopped off for coffee and cake at 20 Mile Hollow—as Graeme and I had done. The weather was perfect for our final farewell. The spot we chose for his ashes was so peaceful and beautiful, with tall trees all around, an enormous rocky outcrop, fresh running water, birds and lizards—nature at its best.

CHAPTER 17

AN UNEXPECTED NEW CHAPTER IN MY LIFE

*T*he months that followed were busy ones for me, as I dealt with the administration of Graeme's estate. The Supreme Court of NSW's website has excellent and detailed information on the steps to be taken, and has application sheets and all the necessary forms to download and print. I'd read through it all during my sleepless overnight periods immediately after Graeme's death. I believed I could manage it all. I saw that the Trustee & Guardian would do this work for $4,400 plus expenses. It took me a while to make a decision but, in early January, when talking to the T and G woman who'd looked after Graeme's finances, I arranged for them to handle it. She said she'd talk to the appropriate person.

I heard nothing further from them. After many frustrating phone calls and emails, I discovered six weeks later that nothing at all had been done. So I decided I would do it myself. I printed out everything. I registered and gave notice of intention to apply for a Grant of Letters of Administration, which would then allow me to open a bank account for Graeme's estate, and have his assets deposited there.

There were so many forms. Forms to prove he had no spouse or de-facto or children. I had to 'search for a will' by writing to his bank, the Trustee & Guardian, and the Supreme Court. The death certificate was needed, and it took a long time coming. When it did, it showed no cause of death, as the coroner had not yet completed the necessary tests. Eventually we learned Graeme died from blood clots in his lungs, as a result of thrombosis in his legs due to the broken ankles. I had to obtain copies of Richard's death certificate from England and his and Graeme's birth certificates. I contacted more people—including the taxation department, the debtors and superannuation companies. (The management costs for the super turned out to be greater than his super payments.)

I began very efficiently, and I didn't find this work upsetting in any way. But I came to a stage where I'd sit at the computer and feel overwhelmed by it all. I mentioned it to Judy one day. I already had information on local solicitors who could do the whole thing. Judy suggested I hand it over, and I agreed with her. I felt the relief immediately. It seemed unfortunate that I'd done so much, and the solicitor would be starting from scratch. But it seemed to me that my sense of 'being undeserving' of the money that was coming to me was preventing me from completing the process. I would pass it on to a solicitor in Springwood. I was very happy going to bed that night, the 'burden' gone.

AN UNEXPECTED NEW CHAPTER IN MY LIFE

However, the next morning I woke with the thought, 'Maybe I could finish the whole thing this weekend'. I decided to give it a go, sat at my computer and found myself easily completing it all. So I photocopied the forms, went to a local JP to have everything verified and my signature witnessed, then took it all to the Supreme Court in Sydney. By June the money was in the estate account. I paid my debts to Simon, bought a small secondhand car, made the decision to take Martin on a short cruise the following year, and had a celebratory meal with Judy and Martin at Silk's Brasserie in Leura.

* * *

I hadn't planned on moving house again, even though I could now afford to be closer to the family. But that winter while coming back in the cold and dark after giving piano lessons to my grandsons after school, I realised how much easier it would be if I moved to their area. 'Meadowbank' popped into my mind. The adjoining suburb to theirs, it's on the Parramatta River and has parks and bushland.

I began looking up rental properties there, and also in Parramatta and in Glebe, where my Canberra friend Barbara had a studio apartment that would soon be available for rental. I agreed not to move until September, when my landlords returned from a holiday in Queensland. My 'guidance' said, 'You know so well that you only need to consider/look at/apply for ONE PLACE'. But I became impatient and began inspecting listed properties. The first one I looked at was in Meadowbank, and it was so disappointing that I decided to forget about that area.

JUST AN ORDINARY PERSON

I actually submitted applications for two places in West Ryde. One I hastily withdrew after my Canberra friend's reaction to seeing it online. I valued her opinion, and agreed with her that it didn't have the setting, the outlook or the room layout I'd hoped for. The other one I'd applied for went to another applicant. I loved it and was most disappointed, but had a sense that something better would become available. The following Saturday I travelled down again to give my grandsons their piano lessons and attend five inspections. The third one was right opposite Simon's place. It seemed quite unsuitable, with an extremely steep and long driveway as the only access. The rent, too, was steep, but I felt it was worth a look. Simon and his family came with me. When I went inside and met the agent showing the property, she said, 'This is not the place for you. I'm going next to open a unit at Meadowbank. That one would be perfect for you'.

She gave me a sheet with all the details, and we all did the ten-minute walk and joined the large number of people inspecting the Meadowbank apartment. And that's where I've been living happily for the last eighteen months. Having been prepared to settle for a tiny studio or bedsit, I ended up with a most spacious, light-filled, two-bedroom apartment, with a very large lock-up garage, my own internal laundry and a bath as well as a shower recess (I've always loved a bath, and hadn't had one at home since Barraba). There's a balcony on the western side, where I have a small table and two chairs, pots of herbs and flowers, and a worm-farm Composta garden. On the eastern side, the bedroom's sliding glass door opens onto a long, paved, ground-level patio; there I have the hammock and a large-sized Vegepod.

AN UNEXPECTED NEW CHAPTER IN MY LIFE

I love it here. It's so comfortable. I look out onto beautiful trees and native shrubs full of birds. I'm two minutes from the train and bus, but don't hear or see them. I can so easily get to shopping centres, the city and even the Central Coast to visit Pearl Beach friends.

* * *

The move from Woodford to Meadowbank was different from all previous moves. I took Judy's advice and had the removalists do all the packing. But there was still much for me to do, of course—sorting through everything, deciding what to take, doing all the change-of-address notifications, the electricity arrangements, opening an E-Toll account and getting my first eTag, among others. With the help of the internet and local charity shops, I found homes for the clothes, bags, shoes and jewellery I'd not been wearing, and for the musty furniture I'd had at Pearl Beach. And I gradually 'unmade' and flattened my garden beds (as my Woodford flat was to become a holiday let) giving away strawberry cuttings, decorative plants and various garden supplies.

At 6 am on Wednesday, 29 August 2018, I picked and pulled out the last of my veggies and packed them into my car. By midday, the flat had been emptied and cleaned, and the removalists were ready to go. I drove behind their van to my new home.

* * *

JUST AN ORDINARY PERSON

I've always enjoyed 'setting up house'. I've now lived in over twenty places and this is the twelfth house I've furnished myself. In every case, the items I've taken with me have been cleaned, polished, repainted or repaired and in the best condition. This time I had the opportunity and thrill of choosing many new items—washing machine/dryer, fridge, dining suite, sofa, TV stand, desks, heater and curtains, and also a bed, small dressing table/desk and chairs for the spare room. It took months for everything to be bought and delivered. For many weeks I had just one office chair, an old upright desk and old TV stand in my large living room.

But while my home was looking better every day, I was looking worse—I was gradually having my teeth out! Just before moving I'd been told that I would have to have dentures and a plate, and arrangements had been made for me to have the work done at a NSW public dental clinic just five minutes by bus from my new apartment.

It was first planned for me to have dentures when I was in my twenties. I'd had most of my first teeth out under a general anaesthetic (ether) when I was young. My parents and my father's parents had false teeth all their adult lives, and I had four badly discoloured front teeth. But the specialist I was passed on to refused to extract teeth for cosmetic reasons, and so I was fitted with crowns. For many years I'd asked dentists if I could have my teeth out and dentures fitted, and they'd always said no. But now it was happening, and I looked forward to having it all over and done with in six months at the latest.

AN UNEXPECTED NEW CHAPTER IN MY LIFE

Fourteen months after the extractions began I brought home my new dentures. One week later, when I returned for a check, the dentist said her adjustments to the upper denture were making it worse and a new one would have to be made. The new one wouldn't stay 'up' and a third upper denture was created. On Christmas Day 2019, I had nice, white, even teeth and was comfortable smiling, but it was painful to eat and I was gagging all the time. When by myself, I removed my teeth to eat! A few days later on the phone to Judy, I laughed and they fell out.

'That's not acceptable!' she said. 'Come and see my dental technician. He'll have a look and tell you if your dentures need adjusting or remaking'. So I travelled up the mountains and saw him, and four days later I was wearing a brand-new denture and a totally remodelled plate. I no longer had the perfect-looking pearly whites—he said that my previous ones were the colour of a twenty-one year-old's teeth. But what I now had looked natural, and they were functional and comfortable.

* * *

At the same time the dental work started, I did a series of free online writing workshops through Hay House with a view to self-publishing my verses. By the end of it I had the thought to write a book about my life. I seriously considered signing up for the expensive course that was to follow, but had a sense that I didn't need more information; I just needed to start writing. I decided that in 2019 I would write a book about my experiences with Graeme. I hoped it would be helpful to some of the many parents of people struggling with addictions. I'd thrown away thirty-two years of daily journaling, but trusted that I would remember what I needed to remember.

And then I read that the author Amanda Hampson was able to mentor up to six people for a year using her *Memoir Made Simple* eBook. I immediately applied and was accepted. It was exactly the kind of program and support I needed. Amanda suggested I write about my life in general. So now, in my mid-eighties, my 'twilight years', I'm producing this book.

I've always loved the twilight—that special glowing light that appears twice a day when the sun is just below the horizon. In built-up areas, where the lights have come on and there's still some daylight, the evening twilight can look truly magical. In the country at that time, the sky and trees can be stunningly beautiful. For many years I've looked out most evenings and been struck by the beauty of the twilight.

I know there's a second definition of the word, meaning obscurity, gradual decline or downturn; but that's not the way I look at it. Dame Edna's husband Norm may have declined in his 'twilight home', but I'm thoroughly enjoying my twilight years, as each day I see everything in a new and more beautiful light. And who knows what opportunities and new adventures tomorrow will bring?

EPILOGUE

It is now traditional in Australia to acknowledge the country's first people—the indigenous aboriginal race—before an event or formal occasion. I want to do more than acknowledge them. I live in a country that has the oldest living culture on earth. Before white man's intervention, the Australian aboriginals lived in harmony with all living and non-living things for some 60,000 years.

While I'm not aware of any aboriginal blood in my veins, I've always felt a strong connection to our first race.

When I was very young, my father frequently spoke of his admiration of the aboriginal women and their natural way of giving birth. We used to tease him about it when he told us, yet again, how they just squatted under a tree, gave birth and popped the baby into a kind of sling, before joining the other members of their tribe walking or working. Maybe it was because my own birth had been so unnatural and horrendous but, whatever his reason, I grew up with that memory and with a strong determination to give birth naturally myself when the time came.

At university I read a book about the aboriginal people of Australia, their spirituality, their beliefs and practices, and was absolutely amazed by it. It struck me that these people had all the answers, and we 'invaders' could learn so much from them.

As a music teacher at Abbotsleigh's Junior School, I transcribed an early recording of an aboriginal song and included it in the wide variety of music I chose for the school to learn and perform at a concert for all the parents and friends.

Then when I was fifty-five and living in Katoomba, I went to an aboriginal spirituality camp, inland from Ulladulla on the South Coast of NSW. I spent a week there, living in the open, washing in the nearby river, learning from a Catholic-school-educated aboriginal elder. He taught us about bush tucker, natural plant remedies and first-aid, and showed us how to make our own clap sticks from a wattle tree. I still treasure the clap sticks I made there. The highlight for me, however, were the daily rituals at sunrise and at sunset, where everyone gathered in silence around a totem on the highest point of the site before welcoming and farewelling the day with humming and chanting. Never before (nor since) have I heard such glorious harmonies as we produced at those times, as with eyes closed we each chose any note to sing, changing it if and when we liked. It was quite magical!

While their numbers have been reduced, and much of their wisdom has already been lost, there is still much we can learn from Australia's first race. The words of my Uluru song sum up my views as well as theirs.

IT IS TIME

It is time to realise
that it isn't really wise
to compete and to deplete,
no matter what the gain.

It is time to realise
It's best not to criticise,
but respect, not reject,
every woman, every man.

Chorus: Let us learn from our first race.
Let us look them in the face
and see all the love and wisdom
that is there—for us to share.

It is time to realise
that we all are in disguise.
Deep within, 'neath our skin,
in reality we're one.

It is time to realise,
if we don't want Earth's demise
we must care, we must share—
see the Sacred everywhere. Chorus

www.ingramcontent.com/pod-product-compliance
Lightning Source LLC
Chambersburg PA
CBHW070249010526
44107CB00056B/2402